AA

40 Short Walks in

WEST YORKSHIRE

Produced by AA Publishing
© AA Media Limited 2011

Researched and written by John Manning
Additional material and walks
by John Morrison (updated by Dennis
Kelsall)

Commissioning Editor: David Popey
Series Management: Sandy Draper
Series Design: Tracey Butler
Copy-editor: Chris Bagshaw
Proofreader: Pam Stagg
Picture Researcher: Liz Allen
Internal Repro and Image Manipulation:
Sarah Montgomery
Cartography provided by the Mapping
Services Department of AA Publishing
Production: Lorraine Taylor

Published by AA Publishing (a trading name
of AA Media Limited, whose registered office
is Fanum House, Basing View, Basingstoke,
Hampshire RG21 4EA; registered number
06112600)

 This product includes
mapping data licensed
from the Ordnance Survey® with the
permission of the Controller of Her Majesty's
Stationery Office. © Crown Copyright 2011.
All rights reserved.
Licence number 100021153.

A04616

978-0-7495-6910-5
978-0-7495-6922-8 (SS)

Colour separation by AA Digital

Printed by Oriental Press

Visit AA Publishing at theAA.com/shop

A CIP catalogue record for this book is
available from the British Library.

The contents of this book are believed
correct at the time of printing. Nevertheless,
the publishers cannot be held responsible
for any errors or omissions or for changes
in the details given in this book or for
the consequences of any reliance on the
information it provides. This does not affect
your statutory rights. We have tried to
ensure accuracy in this book, but things do
change and we would be grateful if readers
would advise us of any inaccuracies they
may encounter.

We have taken all reasonable steps to ensure
that these walks are safe and achievable
by walkers with a realistic level of fitness.
However, all outdoor activities involve a
degree of risk and the publishers accept
no responsibility for any injuries caused to
readers whilst following these walks. For
more advice on walking safely see page 144.
The mileage range shown on the front cover
is for guidance only – some walks may be
less than or exceed these distances.

Some of the walks may appear in other AA
books and publications.

Picture credits

The Automobile Association would like
to thank the following photographers,
companies and picture libraries for their
assistance in the preparation of this book.

Abbreviations for the picture credits are as
follows: (t) top; (b) bottom; (l) left; (r) right; (c)
centre; (AA) AA World Travel Library.

3 AA/J A Tims; 7 AA/M Trelawny;
10 © David Speight/Alamy; 18 AA/J A Tims;
36/7 Courtesy of YSP © Jonty Wilde;
48 AA/J A Tims; 70 © Robert Wade/Alamy;
76/7 AA/D Clapp; 81 AA/T Mackie;
97 © Steven Gillis hd9 imaging/Alamy;
104/5 © Nick Cockman/Alamy; 118 © Phil
Portus/Alamy; 140 AA/J A Tims.

Every effort has been made to trace the
copyright holders, and we apologise in
advance for any accidental errors. We would
be happy to apply the corrections in the
following edition of this publication.

Opposite: View from the Chevin Ridge at Surprise View

40 Short Walks in

WEST YORKSHIRE

Contents

Walk		Rating	Distance	Page
26	**Holme**	+++	3.25 miles (5.3km)	94
27	**Bradford**	+++	1.5 miles (2.4km)	98
28	**Holmbridge**	++++	2.5 miles (4km)	101
29	**Halifax**	+++	3 miles (4.8km)	106
30	**Meltham**	++++	2.75 miles (4.4km)	109
31	**Slaithwaite**	+++	1.5 miles (2.2km)	112
32	**Halifax**	++++	3.25 miles (5.3km)	115
33	**Sowerby Bridge**	++++	1.75 miles (2.8km)	119
34	**Marsden**	++++	1.6 miles (2.6km)	122
35	**Luddenden Dean**	++++	1.5 miles (2.4km)	125
36	**Oxenhope**	+++	1.25 miles (2km)	128
37	**Widdop Reservoir**	++++	2.75 miles (4.4km)	131
38	**Hebden Bridge**	++++	2 miles (3.2km)	134
39	**Hardcastle Crags**	++++	3.75 miles (6km)	137
40	**Cragg Vale**	+++	4 miles (6.4km)	141

Rating

Each walk is rated for its relative difficulty compared to the other walks in this book. Walks marked +++ are likely to be shorter and easier with little total ascent. The hardest walks are marked +++

Walking in Safety

For advice and safety tips see page 144.

Introduction

West Yorkshire is a land of contrasts. The wild west, squeezed between the Yorkshire Dales and Peak District National Parks, is an elevated landscape of rolling moors, cleft by wooded cloughs. The gentler east is big sky country, where the farmer and the miner have all made dramatic impressions on terrain that nevertheless retains outstanding green islands among autumn's golden ocean of ripening cereals.

In the west, where the moors are divided by the valleys of rivers such as the Holme, the Colne and the Calder, you can experience a wide variety of territory during a relatively short walk. From the towns and villages along the narrow valley floor, a walker can follow a tumbling stream up a wooded clough, climb through fields and rough pastures, and find themselves on a high, windswept moor within the space of half an hour.

First-class Walking Territory

Parts of West Yorkshire have the highest density of footpaths per square mile to be found in Britain. The Pennine Way, Britain's first National Trail, rambles across the high moors of Kirklees, Calderdale and Bradford on its way from the Peak District to Scotland. The Trans Pennine Trail, which carries walkers, cyclists and riders from the west coast to the east, visits some of the best parts of Leeds and Wakefield.

England's first Recreational Footpath (if National Trails are the Premier League, then Recreational Footpaths represent the Championship), the Calderdale Way, also belongs to West Yorkshire. In fact West Yorkshire is riddled with high quality walker's trails, including the Kirklees Way, the Leeds Country Way and the Brontë Way (which even transgresses into Red Rose territory).

Rich in Wildlife and History

The county has a rich diversity of wildlife, with a large portion of the western moors enjoying the protection of European legislation as a Special Protection Area because of its important ground nesting birds. In the east, around Wakefield particularly, ugly colliery wastelands have been reclaimed and turned into attractive nature reserves.

The county's historical wealth was made in textiles during the Industrial Revolution. Its legacy can be see everywhere, from the remains of water-powered mills in remote valleys, to the giant mid-1800s industrial complexes in towns such as Saltaire and Meltham. Walkers benefit from the legacy of

Opposite: A boat on the Marsden Canal

that era in the form of packhorse trails, the flagged causey paths of which still provide routes across the higher moors, and the tow paths of the canals, which sliced their way under and over the Pennines to link centres of trade.

Welcoming Walkers

Another revolution is fermenting in the county today in the form of the Walkers Are Welcome scheme, which is spreading rapidly across Britain. Devised in charming-yet-pragmatic Hebden Bridge, its hard-earned logo displayed in a shop, pub or restaurant window is a sign that the business welcomes walkers and goes that extra step to look after them. Of 50 or so existing WAW towns, a disproportionately high number – including Ilkley, Marsden, Mytholmroyd, Otley and of course Hebden Bridge – are in West Yorkshire.

Few places are more welcoming than the friendly cafés and pubs where walkers traditionally seek refreshment – try a West Yorkshire-brewed beer, such as Brass Monkey or Goose Eye, or a Marsden-blend cup of tea for a real taste of the area. Many, especially rural establishments, are happy for you to keep your muddy boots on and bring (well-behaved) dogs into the bar areas. Walkers really are welcome in West Yorkshire.

Using the Book

This collection of 40 walks is easy to use. Use the locator map, see opposite, to select your walk, then turn to the map and directions of your choice. The route of each walk is shown on a map and clear directions help you follow the walk. Each route is accompanied by background information about the walk and area.

INFORMATION PANELS

An information panel for each walk details the total distance, landscape, paths, parking, public toilets and any special conditions that apply, such as restricted access or level of dog friendliness. The minimum time suggested for the walk is for reasonably fit walkers and doesn't allow for stops.

ASCENT AND DIFFICULTY

An indication of the gradients you will encounter is shown by the rating ▲▲▲ (no steep slopes) to ▲▲▲ (several very steep slopes). Walks are also rated for difficulty. Walks marked ✚✚✚ are likely to be shorter and easier with little total ascent. The hardest walks are marked ✚✚✚.

MAPS AND START POINTS

There are 40 maps covering the walks. Some walks have a suggested option in the same area. Each walk has a suggested Ordnance Survey map. The start of each walk is given as a six-figure grid reference prefixed by two letters indicating which 100km square of the National Grid it refers to. You'll find more information on grid references on most Ordnance Survey maps.

CAR PARKING

Many of the car parks suggested are public, but occasionally you may find you have to park on the roadside or in a lay-by. Please be considerate when you leave your car, ensuring that access roads or gates are not blocked and that other vehicles can pass safely.

DOGS

We have tried to give dog owners useful advice about how dog friendly each walk is. Please respect other countryside users. Keep your dog under control, especially around livestock, and obey local bylaws and other dog control notices. Remember, it is against the law to let your dog foul in public areas, especially in villages and towns.

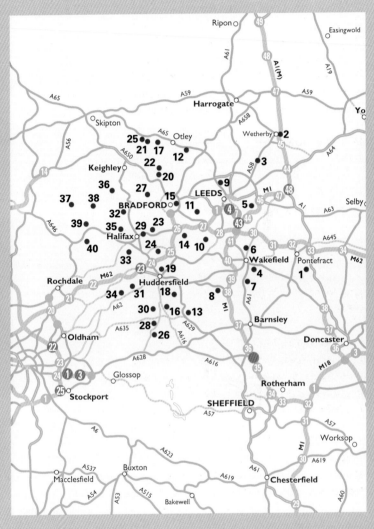

KEY TO WALKING MAPS

--→--	Walk Route	▨	Built-up Area
❶	Route Waypoint	▨	Woodland Area
- - - -	Adjoining Path	🚻	Toilet
⁔⁄	Viewpoint	🅿	Car Park
•	Place of Interest	⊞	Picnic Area
⌂	Steep Section	)(	Bridge

WENT HILL AND WAYWARD WENTBRIDGE

One of West Yorkshire's lowest hills offers one
of the most all-encompassing views.

The charming village of Wentbridge, where the walk begins, has not always
been the tranquil place it is today. Centuries ago, before the development
of the road network, the area was remote and cut-off from society at large.
Nearby Broc-a-Dale – now the Yorkshire Wildlife Trust's Brockadale Nature
Reserve – was regarded as a hive of vagabonds, poachers and misfits,
including cave dweller Mary Pannal, who was convicted of witchcraft at York
in 1603 and burned at Mary Pannal Hill, Ledsham. Her ghost is said to haunt
nearby woodlands. A more famous Wentbridge inhabitant was Robin Hood.
One of the very earliest published legends of the outlaw from around 1500,
A Gest of Robyn Hood, refers to the village and surrounding area directly.

The Great North Road

The arrival in Wentbridge of the Great North Road, the important highway
between York and Edinburgh, brought it rudely into contact with the outside
world and four inns sprang up to cater for the coaching trade. The way out
of the village was feared by coachmen: the steep ascent north, of Went Hill
– regarded as the second steepest on the entire highway after Alnwick in
Northumberland – was tough on their horses.

The road was improved in the 1830s, when a great cutting was made
through the hill, and the only trace that remains of that feared section of
Great North Road today is a crudely surfaced bridleway which parallels the
start of this walk as it climbs out of the village. Not long after the cutting was
dug, the development of the railway network saw the coaching business go
into decline.

The A1 superseded the Great North Road in the 1920s, and high-volume
traffic was taken away from the village altogether in the 1960s when it was
bypassed by the Wentbridge A1 viaduct, built at a cost of £800,000.

One of the coaching inns, survives however. The Bluebell Inn, dating back
to at least 1603, is believed to be the oldest licensed house on the former
great highway. It was substantially rebuilt in 1972 but part of its original
400-year-old inn sign still hangs on a wall inside.

Opposite: Wentbridge is surrounded by rape

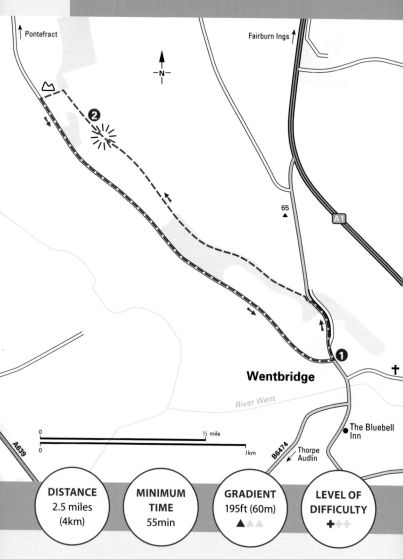

↑ Pontefract

Fairburn Ings ↑

—N—

②

65 ▲

A1

①

Wentbridge

River Went

A639

B6474

Thorpe Audlin ↙

● The Bluebell Inn

✝

0 ————————— ½ mile
0 ————————————— 1km

DISTANCE
2.5 miles
(4km)

MINIMUM TIME
55min

GRADIENT
195ft (60m)
▲ ▲ ▲

LEVEL OF DIFFICULTY
✚ ✚ ✚

PATHS Woodland and field-edge paths, quiet lanes, 1 stile
LANDSCAPE Quiet woodland and ridge above arable countryside
SUGGESTED MAP OS Explorer 278 Sheffield & Barnsley
START/FINISH Grid reference: SE 487174
DOG FRIENDLINESS Dogs should be on lead along roads and near livestock, and under close control elsewhere **PARKING** Park considerately in Wentbridge village **PUBLIC TOILETS** None on route

WALK 1 DIRECTIONS

❶ Walk uphill out of the village on the road towards the A1. Turn left, 90yds (82m) after the pavement expires, on a signed public footpath that leads, up a few crumbling steps, into woodland. It ascends gently to follow a field-edge within the woodland boundary, stepping on to the field margin only briefly to bypass a long-fallen tree. The path eventually leaves the woodland to flirt with the ridge edge; here, out of the trees, the views begin to open up – Emley Moor television transmitter and the hills of the Peak District line the horizon, beyond a landscape of thousands of ploughed acres. Ignore a fork right, up to a gate, and keep walking ahead, past a redundant wooden stile nestling among some shrubs.

🦋 ON THE WALK

The bright orange berries of the female lords and ladies plant, which cluster around the top of a single short stem, are easy to spot on the woodland floor in autumn. Known by many other names, including cuckoo pint, Adam and Eve and Jack in the pulpit, all parts of the plant are poisonous.

❷ A mile (1.6km) after leaving the road, you'll notice a crumbling concrete block in a field to your right. This is the highest point on the walk and a good point at which to decide on your return route to Wentbridge. Your first option is to continue ahead for 186yds (170m), bear left at two successive forks and then descend steeply, through scrub, to reach a wooden step stile into a minor road; turn left along this to return to the village. The other option is to simply retrace your steps along the ridge, this time enjoying the expansive views to the east, which include the power stations at Ferry Bridge, Eggborough and Drax, towards the east coast.

🍴 EATING AND DRINKING

The Bluebell Inn in Wentbridge, the last of the village's four coaching inns, today extends the same welcome to walkers that it once offered to coachmen. The hearty menu includes children's portions. Dogs are welcome on the patio and in the beer garden.

🌿 IN THE AREA

Fairburn Ings, a Royal Society for the Protection of Birds (RSPB) reserve 6 miles (9.7km) north of Wentbridge along the A1, is a fantastic place to spot wetland birds such as reed warbler, green sandpiper and kingfisher, as well as seasonal visitors such as black-tailed godwit and peregrine falcon. The reserve has a visitor centre and laid-out trails. Spring is a great time to visit, children will love pond-dipping or mini-beasting and there is plenty to see on the nestbox cam and in the heronry.

WETHERBY AND THE RIVER WHARFE

Around a handsome country market town and along a stretch of the mature River Wharfe.

Wetherby has a long history and grew up around a tight curve in the River Wharfe. Its importance as a river crossing was recognised by the building of a castle, possibly in the 12th century, of which only the foundations remain. The first mention of a bridge was in 1233. A few years later, in 1240, the Knights Templar were granted a royal charter to hold a market in Wetherby.

At Flint Mill, passed on this walk, flints were ground for use in the pottery industry of Leeds. The town also had two corn mills, powered by water from the River Wharfe. The distinctive, restored weir helped to maintain a good head of water to turn the waterwheels. In general though, the Industrial Revolution made very little impression on Wetherby.

An Ideal Situation

The town grew in importance not from what it made, but from where it was situated. In the days of coach travel, the 400-mile (644km) trip between London and Edinburgh was quite an ordeal for passengers and horses alike. And Wetherby, at the half-way point of the journey, became a convenient stop for mail and passenger coaches. The trade was busiest during the second half of the 18th century, when the town had upwards of 40 inns and alehouses. Coaching inns such as the Swan, the Talbot and the Angel catered for weary travellers and provided stabling for the horses. The Angel was known as 'the Halfway House' and had stables for more than a hundred horses. The Great North Road ran across the town's arched bridge, and through the middle of the town. With coaches arriving and departing daily, it must have presented a busy scene.

When the railway arrived in the 1840s, Wetherby's role as a staging post went into decline. The Great North Road was eventually re-routed around the town, and became known simply as the A1. More recently it has been upgraded to motorway status as the A1(M). When Dr Beeching wielded his axe in 1964, Wetherby lost its railway too. Ironically, a town that had once been synonymous with coach travel is now a peaceful backwater, re-inventing itself once again as an upmarket commuter town.

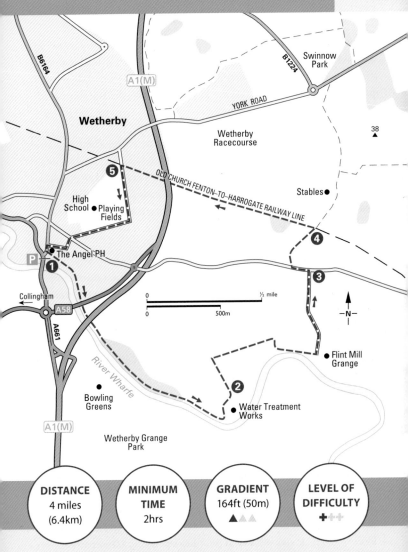

B6164
A1(M)
Wetherby
B1224
Swinnow Park
YORK ROAD
Wetherby Racecourse
38 ▲
Stables ●

DISTANCE	MINIMUM TIME	GRADIENT	LEVEL OF DIFFICULTY
4 miles (6.4km)	2hrs	164ft (50m) ▲▲▲	✚✚✚

PATHS Field paths and good tracks, a little road walking, no stiles

LANDSCAPE Arable land, mostly on the flat

SUGGESTED MAP OS Explorer 289 Leeds

START/FINISH Grid reference: SE 404480

DOG FRIENDLINESS No particular problems

PARKING Free car parking in Wilderness car park, close to river, just over bridge as you drive into Wetherby from south **PUBLIC TOILETS** Wetherby

Walk 2 Wetherby

WALK 2 DIRECTIONS

1 Walk to the far end of the car park, to follow a path at the foot of low cliffs beside the River Wharfe. You pass in quick succession beneath the arches of three modern bridges, carrying the A58 and A1(M) roads across the Wharfe. Emerging beyond, walk the length of a narrow pasture, passing through a kissing gate at the far end by Wetherby's water treatment works.

> ### ♿ ON THE WALK
> Unlike many towns in West Yorkshire, Wetherby still holds its general market every Thursday, with the stalls arranged around the handsome little town hall. Near by are the Shambles, a row of colonnaded stalls built in 1811 to house a dozen butchers' shops.

2 Go left here, up a track around the perimeter fence. After 150yds (137m) you meet a metalled track at the works' main entrance; go left here. At the top of an incline, where the track bears slightly to the right, there is a choice of routes. Your path is sharp right, along a grassy track between fields. You soon approach the wooded slope

that overlooks the River Wharfe. Carry on beside the line of trees towards a farm, Flint Mill Grange. Entering the farmyard, take the farm access road to the left.

3 Meet Walton Road and walk left for 75yds (69m); then go right, along a metalled drive (this is signed as both a bridleway and the entrance to Wetherby Racecourse). After 0.25 miles (400m) you reach a gate.

4 Turn left, dropping onto the trackbed of the old Church Fenton-to-Harrogate railway line, which carried its last train in 1964. A mile's (1.6km) easy walking takes you to the A1(M) motorway, raised up on an embankment as it skirts around Wetherby. Take the underpass beneath the road, and keep ahead along Freemans Way, until you meet Hallfield Lane.

5 Walk left, along Hallfield Lane, following it right around the playing fields of Wetherby High School towards the town centre. At the end, bear left into Nags Lane, right along Victoria Street then go left back to the river.

> ### 🍴 EATING AND DRINKING
> As a market town, and a staging post on the Great North Road, Wetherby is well provided with a choice of pubs, cafés and old coaching inns. The Angel on the High Street serves traditional bar meals at very reasonable prices and has good facilities for children. It's open all day, as is the nearby Red Lion, which also serves a range of good food.

BARDSEY AND POMPOCALI

A rolling landscape with echoes of a Roman past.

The Romans built a network of roads across Yorkshire, which provided good transport links between their most important forts, such as Ilkley (probably their *Olicana*), Tadcaster (*Calcaria*) and York (*Eboracum*). And one of these roads, marked on old maps as Ryknield Street, passed close to Bardsey, continuing west to a small Roman camp established at Adel. You walk a short stretch of the old Roman road from Hetchell Wood, a local nature reserve.

Stirring Remains

Adjacent to these woods – and marked on the Ordnance Survey map as Pompocali – are a set of intriguing earthworks. A number of Roman finds have been unearthed here, including a quern for grinding corn and a stone altar dedicated to the god Apollo. And 2 miles (3.2km) away, at Dalton Parlours, the site of a large Roman villa has been discovered.

Once the Romans had abandoned this northern outpost of their empire, Bardsey became part of the kingdom of Elmet, and was later mentioned in the Domesday Book. By the 13th century, the village had been given to the monks of Kirkstall Abbey. After the Dissolution of Monasteries, in 1539, Bardsey came under the control of powerful local families – notably the Lords Bingley. The Parish Church of All Hallows, visited towards the end of this walk, is another antiquity – the core of the building is Anglo Saxon.

Above the church is a grassy mound, where a castle once stood. Pottery found on the site indicates it was occupied during the 12th and 13th centuries, and then abandoned. Some of the stonework from the castle was incorporated into Bardsey Grange, whose most notable inhabitant was William Congreve. Born here in 1670, Congreve went on to write a number of Restoration comedies, such as *The Way of the World*.

So close to the city, yet retaining its own identity, Bardsey has expanded beyond its ancient centre to become a popular commuter village for people working in Leeds. It joins that elite group of places that lay claim to having the country's oldest pub. The Bingley Arms has better claims than most; there is documentary evidence of brewers and innkeepers going back 1,000 years.

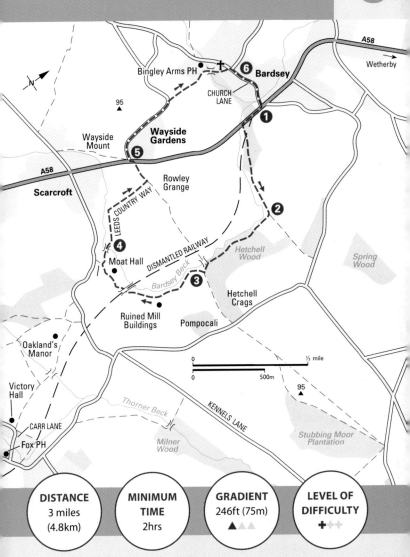

DISTANCE
3 miles
(4.8km)

MINIMUM TIME
2hrs

GRADIENT
246ft (75m)
▲▲▲

LEVEL OF DIFFICULTY
✛✚✚

PATHS Good paths and tracks (though some, being bridleways, may be muddy), 2 stiles **LANDSCAPE** Arable and woodland

SUGGESTED MAP OS Explorer 289 Leeds

START/FINISH Grid reference: SE 368432

DOG FRIENDLINESS Keep on lead around Bardsey and while crossing A58

PARKING Street parking off A58 at southern end of Bardsey

PUBLIC TOILETS None on route

Opposite: Hetchell Crags

WALK 3 DIRECTIONS

1 From the junction of Church Lane with the A58, follow the main road south. After 150yds (137m), turn off left beside a gate along a contained path into woods, soon joining with a path from the left that follows the course of the old railway line between Leeds and Wetherby. A few paces farther on, bear left over a stile. Emerging on to the edge of a field, continue at the perimeter, turning with the corner and walking down to another wood.

2 Pass through a gap to enter Hetchell Wood. Keep right where the path later forks to pass beneath Hetchell Crags. You soon come to a meeting of paths, beside a footbridge over the beck. Don't cross but go left, climbing a short way along a track, which is part of a Roman road, to find a bridleway signed off through a gate on the right.

3 Through the gate, a path leads away above the stream, skirting the Roman earthworks. Beyond an overhanging rock, the path rises to a junction (to the left, you can investigate the camp). The onward path lies to the right through a gateway and past ruined mill buildings. Joining a track, follow it beneath an old railway bridge. Immediately after crossing a stream, go right through a small gate and cross to another in the opposite corner of the field. Walk ahead along a drive from Moat Hall, to a stile breaking the right-hand wall, a few paces along on the right.

4 Take a field-edge path, with a hedge to the right (from here back to Bardsey you are walking the Leeds Country Way). Towards the far end of the field, your path turns right into a copse. Cross a beck on a wooden footbridge and swing left along a hollow way hemmed in by hedgerows. Later emerging into the corner of a field, climb away beside the right-hand hedge. Drop beyond the crest of the hill to a junction. Go left here on a track that follows a broken wall to meet the A58.

5 Walk left for 20yds (18m) and then turn right into Wayside Mount, an unsurfaced access road serving houses. Beyond the last house go through a gate and follow the track ahead, with a tall hedge on your left. When the track swings left, walk ahead down a field-edge path, following a hedge on the left. Bear half right, near the bottom of the field, to join a narrow path through scrubland, over a beck, and up to a gate into the churchyard. Keep right of the church to meet a road.

6 Go right on Church Lane to return to the start point.

---

⑪ EATING AND DRINKING

The Bingley Arms, in Bardsey, is a contender for the title of the oldest pub in England. Parts of the pub are supposed to date back to AD 950, when it was known as the Priests Inn. It has excellent food and, in summer, barbecues on the terrace.

NATURE RECLAIMS WALTON COLLIERY

How nature is being given a helping hand to reclaim a landscape once scarred by mining.

Walton Colliery Nature Reserve is a wonderful example of how a former industrial site, which once scarred the land terribly, can be turned into a haven for wildlife and walkers alike.

At its peak the colliery employed more than 1,000 men but today virtually every trace of the former mine has vanished. The pitheads have gone, along with the miners' bathouse, the store for their lamps, and the railway sidings from which the coal was transported away. The tips have been landscaped, woodland has been planted and the pits are now peaceful lakes, home to geese, ducks, swans and more. Only a little visible spoil from one of the old waste heaps hints that the site was ever an industrial wasteland.

Sharlton West Colliery

The pit was sunk in the late 19th century when better technology enabled the creation of deeper, more productive shafts. The development of the canal and rail networks also meant coal could more easily be sold and transported elsewhere. By 1930, the colliery was one of the country's best-equipped, employing around 1,200 men. In 1978, a year before it closed, that figure had dropped to 740 but the pit still managed to produce 230,000 tons of coal.

The last coal was dug at Walton on December 3, 1979, and work on transforming the degraded area into a 178-acre (72ha) nature park began in 1993. The operation wasn't minor: massive earth moving equipment was brought in to reshape the landscape, the site was covered in topsoil, 100,000 native trees including cherry, oak, willow, ash, birch and hazel were planted, and several lagoons were created, along with 6 miles (9.7km) of paths.

The work was completed by 1996 and the park was designated a Local Nature Reserve in 2008. In 2010 a conservation group, the Friends of Walton Colliery Nature Park, created to help Wakefield Council manage the reserve, began a programme of thinning the maturing shrubs and woodlands.

There are abundant signs that nature is re-occupying the site, from the five-spot Burnett moths on the grasslands, to the herons, toads and dragonflies in the old waterways, and the sparrowhawks that flit through the woodlands.

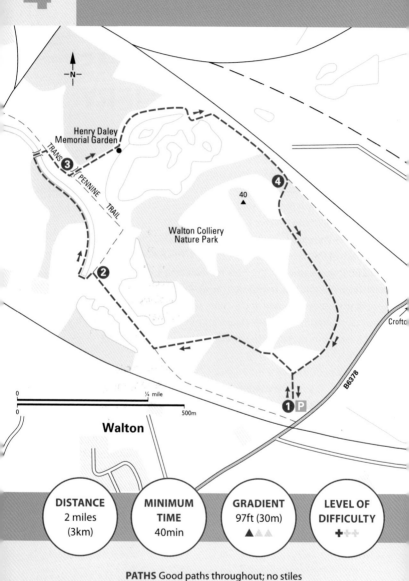

DISTANCE	MINIMUM TIME	GRADIENT	LEVEL OF DIFFICULTY
2 miles (3km)	40min	97ft (30m) ▲▲▲	✚✚✚

PATHS Good paths throughout; no stiles

LANDSCAPE Regenerative woodland, meadow and manmade lakes

SUGGESTED MAP OS Explorer 278 Sheffield & Barnsley

START/FINISH Grid reference: SE 364176

DOG FRIENDLINESS Dogs can exercise freely in the park

PARKING Car park at Walton Colliery Nature Park, Shay Lane, Crofton, Wakefield

PUBLIC TOILETS None on route

WALK 4 DIRECTIONS

❶ Leave the car park on the well-surfaced path that passes between two metal posts, crosses a small stream, then bears left at a fork after 65yds (60m) to ascend to a grassy plateau. Bear left here on a wide path, which gently descends to a gravel vehicle track. Turn right, passing between two lakes. The lake on the right was once the source of clay used to pack explosives into the coal seams.

❷ At a junction, turn left then immediately right to cross a narrow, reed-fringed watercourse and follow it downstream. Look out for grey wagtail, long tailed tit and dragonflies. Re-crossing the stream on a footbridge, turn right along the Trans Pennine Trail, doubling back on the opposite bank to another footbridge over another clear stream to a junction.

❸ Cross the trail here and keep ahead, up a small rise between plantations to pass the Henry Daley Memorial Garden.

---

⑪ EATING AND DRINKING

Walton's New Inn has had a place in the Good Beer Guide for several years. The former coaching inn serves meals every day except Monday and offers a children's menu. Dogs are also welcome in the pub. Four regular hand-lifted ales are offered, including beers from the Leeds Brewery, Black Sheep and Timothy Taylor.

The trail reaches another junction: turn right, over a small bridge, on a track that leads past another large body of water on your right. Ignoring junctions off to the right, parallel the railway to a brow where walkers and trains are on the same level.

❹ Bear right here on an unsurfaced path. Ignore side trails and keep ahead on the well-used path, swinging left when it is joined by another from the right. After rounding a corner, fork left to rejoin your outward path back to the car park.

---

⑫ IN THE AREA

Having sampled the above-ground reclamation of a coal mine, a taste of a miner's life below ground is in order. At the National Coal Mining Museum for England at Caphouse Colliery, in Overton, former miners will take you on an underground guided tour. You can also meet pit ponies and see the country's oldest mine shaft still in daily use.

🐾 ON THE WALK

On the site of a row of miners' cottages known as The Spikes, or Spike Island, there stands a sundial memorial to local Councillor Henry Daley, who died in 1995, a tribute to his commitment to improving the environment for local people. Each of the hours passed by the shadow of an 8ft (2.4m) obelisk is marked, appropriately, by a spike.

TEMPLE NEWSAM'S STATELY COUNTRYSIDE

Explore a tranquil 'Capability Brown' landscape
just a short distance from Leeds city centre.

Temple Newsam is one of England's finest historic houses. The parklands were laid out by Lancelot 'Capability' Brown in the late 1760s for Charles Ingram and today its lakes, woodlands and formal gardens, in the care of Leeds City Council, are available for all to explore.

The earliest record of the property is in the Domesday Book as 'Neuhusam', meaning 'new house'. The preface 'Temple' comes from the fact that it was owned by the Knights Templar between 1155 and 1307, when the order was quashed following Papal decree and the property seized by the state.

Sir Arthur Ingram

Subsequent owners faired little better until 1622, when Sir Arthur Ingram bought the estate and built the basis of the mansion we see today. Regarded by some as a wise financier and by others a rogue, the native of Rothwell made his fortune during the struggle to make James I and Charles I financially independent of parliament. He was knighted in 1613 and became one of the most powerful men in the county of Yorkshire.

His descendants remodelled various wings over subsequent decades and in the 1760s Charles Ingram, the ninth Viscount of Irvine, commissioned 'Capability Brown' to remodel the estate.

Much of 'Capability Brown's' design survives today. He opted for a natural design, breaking up the symmetry imposed by the house and opening up fresh vistas to the west and south. Functional buildings, such as stables, were screened by fresh tree planting and a new approach along a long driveway, which passed between gates guarded by sphinxes, was created.

It was during this period that the Prince of Wales, later to become George IV, presented Ingram's daughter, Lady Hertford, his mistress, with a pair of 18th-century Brussels tapestries depicting biblical stories. These, and many other great works of art, including furniture masterpieces by Thomas Chippendale, silver and Leeds pottery, are on display within the house.

Today the estate offers even more to the people of Leeds, with classical and pop concerts, cycling, riding, golf and of course walking.

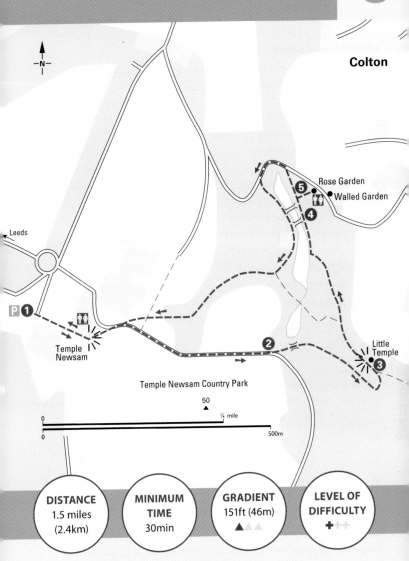

Colton

Leeds

Rose Garden

Walled Garden

Temple
Newsam

Little
Temple

Temple Newsam Country Park

50 ▲

¼ mile

500m

DISTANCE	MINIMUM TIME	GRADIENT	LEVEL OF DIFFICULTY
1.5 miles (2.4km)	30min	151ft (46m) ▲▲▲	✚✚✚

PATHS Good tracks and paths throughout; no stiles

LANDSCAPE Parkland, gardens, lakes and woodland

SUGGESTED MAP OS Explorer 289 Leeds

START/FINISH Stable Courtyard, Temple Newsam Grid reference: SE 357321

DOG FRIENDLINESS Dogs should be under control; please clear up after them

PARKING Pay-and-display in the House Car Park, off Temple Newsam Road, Leeds

PUBLIC TOILETS In Stable Courtyard at start and at the Rose Garden

WALK 5 DIRECTIONS

❶ Leave the car park and pass by the left side of the main house. Bear left and follow the main track that sweeps downhill below the Stable Courtyard. Fork right beyond the estate buildings, down to a junction by a pond.

❷ Leave the hard-surfaced track here and take the narrow path ahead, signed for the Little Temple, across a patch of grass and over the pond's outflow into woodland. The edged path rises to follow the right edge of a clearing, to a junction.

> **🍴 EATING AND DRINKING**
>
> Having visited the rare breeds on the Home Farm, you can enjoy a taste of them in the Temple Newsam Tea Room in the Stable Courtyard. The café serves snacks, afternoon teas and hot meals, and focuses on local produce including its own sausages and burgers. It is closed on Mondays during winter.

path. Bear right, then left down the brick-surfaced track met at a crossroads, to the water's edge.

❹ Turn right past two wooden footbridges to a fork. Here, your route continues ahead left but a diversion to the right, to explore the Rose Garden and Georgian Walled Garden, will more than repay the minimal effort involved.

> **⚓ ON THE WALK**
>
> On a hillside gazing across to Temple Newsam House, you'll find the Little Temple, created in the 18th century to enhance the already splendid view from the house. Supported by four classical columns it, in turn, offers an excellent view back across the valley to the house.

❺ Returning to the junction, resume your earlier direction. Bear hard left at the next opportunity to double back down the opposite side of the lakes, past the two footbridges. The trail sweeps up to a junction and bears right to wind its way back to the house, stables and car park beyond.

❸ Turn left here, past the Little Temple on the path signed 'Easy going path to lakes'. This gently descends through rhododendron, zig-zagging at the bottom to a junction with the lakeside

> **🌿 IN THE AREA**
>
> Temple Newsam's Home Farm was the maintenance base for the grand estate in years gone-by. Today, visitors are welcome to explore its cobbled yards, admire its 17th-century Great Barn and delight in Europe's largest rare breeds farm, which has more than 400 animals including sheep, poultry (don't miss the Transylvanian naked neck hen), cattle, goats and pigs.

STANLEY MARSH – A WILDLIFE OASIS

A tiny oasis of natural calm little more than a mile from the city centre.

Stanley Marsh hasn't always been a marsh. Maps of the area from more than 200 years ago show an area of fields where the tiny tarn now sits. Over the last half-century, a combination of subsidence from coal mining and the blocking of field drains has caused the area to flood, creating the tarn and wetlands.

Today the site is managed by the Friends of Stanley Marsh, together with Wakefield Council's countryside rangers. There's a path around the tarn and through its surrounding woodlands, as well as a viewing platform on the water's edge. A hay meadow on the perimeter of the reserve is alive in springtime with wild flowers and butterflies, including the common blue, speckled wood and comma species, while the same time of year sees the tarn become a breeding ground for amphibians such as frogs and newts. Throughout the year resident birds including green woodpecker, kingfisher, heron and sparrowhawks can be seen.

Deep Drop Pit

The warden's hut in Lime Pit Lane stands on the site of a spa discovered in 1826, when a 240ft (73m) bore was dug to test the area's potential for coal mining. Sunk in 1835 and known locally as Deep Drop Pit, the shaft was the deepest of five that made up Stanley Victoria Colliery and little remains of it today: if you search hard you might find the pit's overgrown outline. Another clue to the site's industrial past is the walk's only real incline, up which a few steps have been built. This highest point, just a few feet above the tarn's shore, is what's left of a raised tram bank, built to ferry coal from the pit to nearby Bottom Boat where it could be distributed by the canal network, via the Aire and Calder Navigation.

Pit ponies were grazed in the fields before the colliery was closed in 1879 after an underground explosion killed 21 men, including five boys. The landscape reverted to fields before subsidence and flooding changed the character of the landscape again.

Trees planted in the memory of the miners who died in the 1879 blast were replaced when the reserve was created.

Stanley

Leeds

Stanley Marsh

Wildflower Meadow

A642

Stanley Ferry, Wakefield

220 yds

250m

DISTANCE	MINIMUM TIME	GRADIENT	LEVEL OF DIFFICULTY
1 mile (1.6km)	20min	22ft (7m)	

PATHS Engineered woodland path, good field path; no stiles
LANDSCAPE Wooded pond and wetland, wildflower meadow
SUGGESTED MAP OS Explorer 289 Leeds **START/FINISH** Grid reference:
SE 346236 **DOG FRIENDLINESS** Dogs are free to wander but should be under
close control during the nesting season between March and July **PARKING** Car
park, Lime Pit Lane, Stanley, Wakefield **PUBLIC TOILETS** None on route
NOTE Parts of the path around the reserve are suitable for assisted wheelchair
users – RADAR key required

WALK 6 DIRECTIONS

❶ Before starting your walk it's worth noticing the warden's hut in the car park in Lime Pit Lane. It stands on the site of a spa discovered in 1826, when a 240ft (73m) bore was dug to test the area's potential for coal mining. Spa Fold Cottages were built to accommodate those coming to bathe in the red-stained waters, purported to have medicinal qualities. The business didn't last long – the development of a coal pit led to the water being pumped away and the spa drying up. From the car park, enter the reserve through the metal kissing gate and bear right at a junction encountered just beyond. At a second junction 330yds (302m) later, keep left over a stream, past a wetland area on your right.

❷ Bear right at the next junction, to exit the woodland, then immediately left along the edge of the wildflower meadow. This soon slips back beneath trees and brings you to a crossroads of paths close to Lime Pit Lane.

❸ Climb the bank ahead-left for the best views across the water; there is a wooden viewing platform to your left, an ideal spot from which to get close to the ducks and swans.

❹ Descend steps on the far side of the mound and fork right a few paces beyond, back into the car park.

> ### 🐦 ON THE WALK
> An insistent 'tsee tsee tsee' call could alert you to the presence of family flocks of long-tailed tits among the bushes. The bird constructs an elaborate, egg-shaped home of lichen, moss and spiders' webs – in abundant supply here – then camouflages it with bark and lines the interior with a thousand tiny feathers.

> ### 🍴 EATING AND DRINKING
> The Stanley Ferry pub, at the entrance to the marina in Ferry Lane, regularly welcomes parties of walkers. Recently renovated, it offers a traditional menu seven days a week between noon and 10pm, as well as a children's menu. There's a children's play area, known as the Wacky Warehouse, and a beer garden in which dogs are welcome.

> ### 🌿 IN THE AREA
> The Aire and Calder Navigation, along which coal from Deep Drop Pit was carried, boasts one of the wonders of the inland waterways network. Opened in 1839 and still in use today, the Stanley Ferry Aqueduct is believed to be the world's largest cast iron aqueduct. Its span of 165ft (50m) carries the canal over the River Calder and was designed by George Leather Senior.

A WALK AROUND NEWMILLERDAM

A pleasant oasis, close to Wakefield,
and a chance to feed the ducks.

Newmillerdam Country Park lies on the A61 near the village of Newmillerdam, and 3 miles (4.8km) south of Wakefield. The name refers, unsurprisingly, to a 'new mill on the dam' – a mill where people brought their corn to be ground was built in the area in around 1285, at which point the area cast off its old Norse name of Thurstonhaugh.

The Chevet Estate

The lake and woods were created as a park for a 16th-century country house, which was demolished in the 1960s due to the effects of mining subsidence. From 1753, the park formed part of the Chevet Estate, which was owned by the Pilkington family. They used the lake for fishing and shooting and, in 1820, built a distinctive boathouse, close to the site of the original 13th-century mill, as a place for their guests to socialise and enjoy the lake view. This restored Grade II listed building is now used as a visitor centre. Gamekeepers protected the wildfowl and fish from poachers and two of the lodges built to house them in the 1870s still stand by the gates at either end of the dam.

A Public Park

In 1954 Newmillerdam was sold to the council and, two years later, opened to all as a public park. Local people come here to walk, fish, watch birds or just feed the ducks. The lake is surrounded by woodland. Conifer trees were planted during the 1950s with the intention, once the trees had reached maturity, of using the wood for making pit props for the coal mines. These trees are mature now but, ironically, the need for pit props has gone as all but one of Yorkshire's pits have closed. Wakefield Council's Countryside Service is gradually replacing the conifers with broadleaved trees such as oak, ash, birch and hazel, which support a greater variety of birdlife.

A simple circuit of the lake is a pleasant 2-mile (3.2km) stroll, on a track suitable for buggies or wheelchairs, and is very popular. This walk takes you just a little further, away from the crowds into quieter woodland at the far end of the lake.

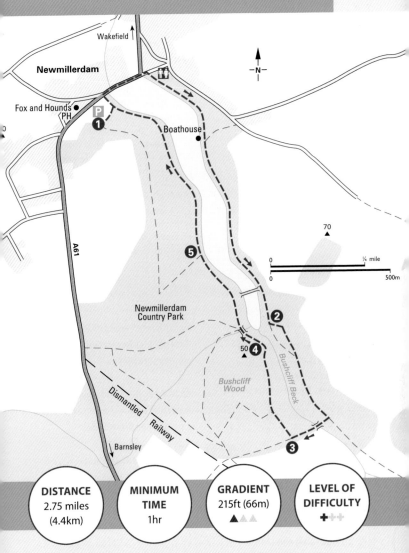

DISTANCE
2.75 miles
(4.4km)

MINIMUM TIME
1hr

GRADIENT
215ft (66m)

LEVEL OF DIFFICULTY

PATHS Good paths by lake and through woodland; no stiles
LANDSCAPE Reservoir and mixed woodland **SUGGESTED MAP** OS Explorer
278 Sheffield & Barnsley **START/FINISH** Grid reference: SE 330157
DOG FRIENDLINESS Can run free throughout once off the road
PARKING Pay-and-display car park at western end of dam, on A61
between Wakefield and Barnsley
PUBLIC TOILETS At opposite end of dam wall from car park

WALK 7 DIRECTIONS

❶ Walk right, along the A61, to the far side of the lake, to join a path down the eastern side of the lake. Pass the ornate boathouse and a causeway across the lake.

❷ Where the lake narrows to a beck, bear left, rising gently to a junction at which you swing right, descending again almost imperceptibly. At a crossroads of paths (or at the slightly earlier fork) turn right, across Bushcliff Beck beyond which the path rises past a small group of conifers to another junction.

🦆 ON THE WALK

Ducks, geese and swans have no trouble finding food at Newmillerdam, as people with bagfuls of stale bread queue to feed them. The most common of the ducks you'll see is the mallard, the 'basic' duck. The females are brown and make the satisfying 'quack quack' sounds which delight children. The males have distinctive green heads, yellow bills and grey bodies. Their tone is more nasal and much weaker sounding. Mallards pair off in late autumn but the males leave egg incubation and rearing of the young to the females.

🌍 IN THE AREA

Immediately to the north of Newmillerdam is Pugneys Country Park, a popular place of recreation. A large lake is overlooked by what remains of Sandal Castle. The original motte and bailey date from the 12th century, the later stone castle from the days of Richard III. He had planned to make Sandal Castle his key permanent stronghold in the north before he was killed at the Battle of Bosworth in 1485.

❸ Turn right into Bushcliff Wood, then right at the next fork down to another junction.

❹ Turn left here, and stay with the waterside path at a fork just beyond a small stone footbridge.

❺ Stay with this well surfaced path all the way up the west side of the lake, forking right at the far end to return to the car park.

🍴 EATING AND DRINKING

Ideally sited near Newmillerdam's car park, the Fox and Hounds pub welcomes families, serving meals (including a children's menu) all week, with the exception of Sunday evening. Dogs are permitted in the bar area, where three Yorkshire-brewed cask ales are served. If lighter refreshment is required, the Beuley Café stands opposite the dam wall, and is open until 4pm every day except Monday. Elsewhere in Newmillerdam you'll find a curry restaurant, a Toby Carvery, and an Italian restaurant tucked discreetly away in the corner of the dam's car park.

OUTDOOR ART AT BRETTON COUNTRY PARK

A visit to a fine estate that's been transformed
into an acclaimed contemporary sculpture park.

Bretton Hall is a fine 18th-century mansion by Sir William Wentworth,
who was inspired to build in a grand Palladian style after a Grand Tour of
Europe. He sited his house on a hill, to enjoy the view across his two lakes
and landscaped parkland. Bretton Hall college, recently merged with the
University of Leeds, now has a new role as an educational campus. In these
tranquil surroundings, students can study arts, music and performance.

A Thoroughly Modern Exhibition

The Yorkshire Sculpture Park was established in 1977, the first such venture
in Britain. Exhibitions of modern and contemporary art are displayed in over
500 acres (202ha) of parkland, together with four indoor galleries, providing
a changing programme of exhibitions, displays and projects. More than
200,000 people a year visit this 'art gallery without walls'. This walk explores
some of its quieter corners, discovering major works away from the main
galleries. Both Bretton Country Park and the neighbouring sculpture park are
open year-round, and entrance is free.

Henry Moore was one of the first to sculpt works for informal settings,
where they would be encountered by people unlikely to visit a gallery. More
than a dozen of his bronze figures – monumental in scale, yet recognisably
human – have found a permanent home in Bretton Country Park. Moore,
born in nearby Castleford, studied at Leeds School of Art and remained close
to his roots, even when his renown took on global proportions.

Barbara Hepworth was another whose work helped define modern art.
Born in 1903 in Wakefield, she was a contemporary of Moore's; the two
studied together in Leeds and at the Royal College of Art, in London. You'll
find her *Family of Man* series of nine works in the Sculpture Park's Hillside area.
Hepworth's most significant public work stands outside the United Nations
Secretariat in New York: 1964's *Single Form* was commissioned in memory
of UN secretary general Dag Hammarskjöld. From 1950 until her death in a
fire 25 years later she lived and worked in St Ives, Cornwall. A major new art
gallery celebrating her work opened in Wakefield in 2011.

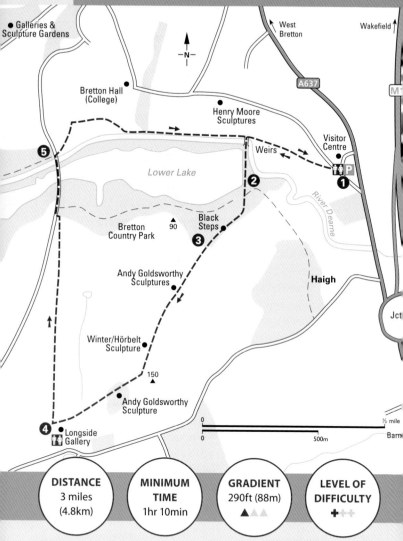

WALK 8 DIRECTIONS

❶ Pass through kissing gates left of the visitor centre on to a grassy path that soon meets a track. Bear right, then immediately left downhill across an open field. After meeting a fence on the left, turn left over Dam Head Bridge, past a cascading weir, and continue ahead over the dam wall of the Lower Lake.

❷ At a fork by an ornate well, bear right for 44yds (40m), then left to ascend Oxley Bank on sculptor David Nash's flight of Black Steps. Follow the path along the edge, taking care over exposed tree roots. The walk along Oxley Bank is interrupted only briefly by a short flight of stone steps and subsequent re-ascent of the opposite bank.

❸ Turn right through a stone gap stile to continue the walk along the bank, past a permanent series of Andy Goldsworthy sculptures entitled *Hanging Trees*. Beyond Wolfgang

Winter and Berthold Hörbelt's *Basket #7* sculpture, the path sweeps right and descends through the Round Garden, past another Goldsworthy sculpture. Cross to the corner of the subsequent field and take the cinder track beyond, ahead-right, to the Longside Gallery.

> ### 🖉 IN THE AREA
> Allow extra time to explore in full the Yorkshire Sculpture Park and its galleries. The walk passes the Longside Gallery; on the other side of the park, 1.25 miles (2km) away, is the Underground Gallery, which hosts major exhibitions by internationally acclaimed contemporary and modern artists, the nearby Bothy Gallery, and the Garden Gallery, as well as an outdoor sculpture trail suitable for wheelchairs and prams.

❹ Past the gallery turn right through a gate in the fence and descend the field to the bottom right corner, following the fence on your right its entire length. Turn left on the track met in the corner for 65yds (60m), then pass through wrought iron gates between decorative posts to cross the Upper Lake's dam wall and the River Dearne.

> ### 🍴 EATING AND DRINKING
> A licensed restaurant and coffee shops in the Yorkshire Sculpture Park Centre offers the chance for a sit down, a light snack and leisurely views of the artworks on display throughout the park. If you're seeking reliable pub food, try the Black Bull at Midgley, between West Bretton and Flockton. It's a Brewer's Fayre pub with a cosy atmosphere, and serves meals all day.

❺ Turn right at a crossroads on a good track, below Bretton Hall, then bear right, down a lane. Turn left on a cinder track before a bridge and pass through a gate back into the country park. Follow the grassy track, past a series of Henry Moore sculptures and Dam Head Bridge, to the car park.

Molecule Man 1+1+1 by Jonathan Borofsky at the Yorkshire Sculpture Park

MEANWOOD'S RURAL GREEN CORRIDOR

From the bustle of the city to the wild side of Leeds.

This, the only linear walk in the book, is a splendid ramble, surprisingly rural in aspect throughout, even though it begins just a stone's throw from the bustling heart of the city of Leeds. You start among the terraces of red-brick houses that are so typical of the city, and five minutes later you are in delightful woodland.

The Dales Way and the Meanwood Valley Trail

Sections of this route follow the first few miles of both the Dales Way Link Path between Leeds and Ilkley (the Dales Way's official starting point) and the Meanwood Valley Trail, so there are regular waymarkers to keep you on track until you leave Meanwood Park.

The 7-mile (11.3km) Meanwood Valley Trail links the city centre with Breary Marsh in Golden Acre Park, where it meets the Leeds Country Way. It is also the setting for the Meanwood Valley Trail Race, held every year since 1996 and which attracts more than 300 runners. Organised by the Meanwood Valley-based Valley Striders Athletic Club the race, together with the Baildon Boundary Way and the Guiseley Gallop, forms part of a series known as the Airedale Triple Trail Series.

The Meanwood Valley Trail, the Dales Way Link and this walk all begin by the statue of philanthropist Henry Rowland Marsden, said to have been Victorian Leeds' most popular mayor. He looks out across Woodhouse Moor, where fairs and circuses have traditionally pitched their tents for centuries.

The path follows Woodhouse Ridge and the Meanwood Valley into Meanwood Park, cocooned against creeping suburbia by a slim but beautiful sliver of woodland, a vital corridor for wildlife. Leeds is fortunate to have so many parks within its city limits: long-established green spaces such as Roundhay Park, and newer parks created from 'brownfield' sites. Meanwood Park is a 71.5-acre (29ha) open space which includes a bowling green, tennis courts and children's play area. It is thought that the Leeds-born Victorian landscape artist John Atkinson Grimshaw might have set some of his paintings within its delightful environs.

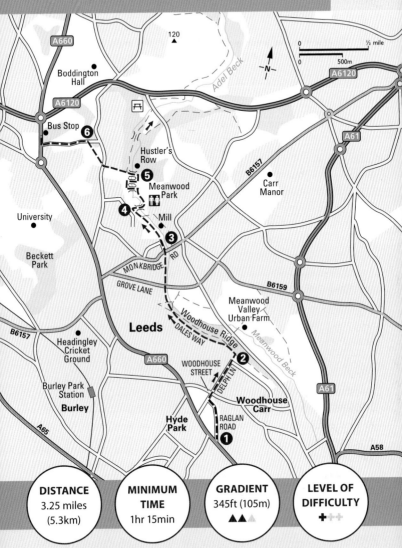

DISTANCE
3.25 miles
(5.3km)

MINIMUM TIME
1hr 15min

GRADIENT
345ft (105m)
▲▲▲

LEVEL OF DIFFICULTY
✚✚✚

PATHS Urban ginnels (alleys), parkland and woodland paths; 1 stile
LANDSCAPE Woodland, parkland and urban fringe
SUGGESTED MAP OS Explorer 289 Leeds **START** Grid reference: SE 292350
FINISH Opposite Lawnside School, Otley Road, Leeds; grid reference: SE 268379
DOG FRIENDLINESS Good but watch for traffic when encountering roads
PARKING Street parking around Raglan Road off the A660, opposite Hyde Park
PUBLIC TOILETS Slightly off-route, shortly after entering Meanwood Park
NOTE A regular bus service returns to the starting point

WALK 9 DIRECTIONS

❶ Walk down the length of Raglan Road (opposite The Library, a public house at the corner of Hyde Park) and turn right on to Rampart Road. Cross Woodhouse Street, and walk ahead up Delph Lane.

❷ When the road ends after 550yds (503m), take a gate on the left. Through this, bear left on the higher path along Woodhouse Ridge. Keep ahead at the first junction, where steps rise from the right, and ignore other trails off to the right to follow a high wall along the ridge, eventually descending to a barrier. Where the trail splits, take the middle option, signed to Grove Lane. There, cross carefully and follow the continuing path opposite, crossing another track after 200yds (183m) and emerging soon after in Monkbridge Road.

❸ Cross the road and take Highbury Lane, crossing Highbury Mount at the end to recover the path ahead, which now accompanies Meanwood Beck. As you pass a mill, fork first left, then turn right, above the mill dam. Walk through Hollin Lane Allotments and out along a rough track to meet a quiet residential road.

❹ Without setting foot on the road, turn right, over a small stone footbridge on a path by an old watercourse, to cross a second footbridge. Turn immediate left

there, through a gap in the wall, into Meanwood Park. Follow the good path ahead, signed 'Meanwood Valley Trail', through a crossroads to cross Meanwood Beck on either of two stone footbridges, continuing upstream to cross an arched stone-built bridge. Turn left to leave the park through a gap in the wall, into a rough lane below Hustler's Row.

❺ Turn left, recross the beck on a footbridge and keep ahead up a path which soon joins Weetwood Mill Lane to rise to Weetwood Lane. Cross Weetwood Lane and bear right. Just past the grand gateway to Bardon Hall, turn left, between iron bollards, along a narrow walled path.

> 🍽 **EATING AND DRINKING**
> There are plenty of options in Leeds but, if you'd rather avoid the city, just a few strident paces to the right before crossing Monkbridge Road will take you to Meanwood. There you'll find East of Arcadia, the menu of which is described as 'new British'. There's a children's menu and dogs are welcome.

❻ At the far end, cross the lane and the small stone step stile almost directly opposite. Turn left, to walk between Leeds University residences and sports pitches, finally emerging into Otley Road. Walk right to find a bus stop, just past the entrance to Weetwood Hall Hotel, for the bus back to Woodhouse Moor.

THE RUINS OF HOWLEY HALL

One of Yorkshire's finest mansions was demolished three centuries ago but the view it commanded still impresses.

Little remains above ground today of the splendid Tudor mansion that once stood between the towns of Morley and Batley. Nevertheless Howley Hall was a magnificent structure, one of the finest Elizabethan houses in Yorkshire. It commanded the visual attention of a wide area, standing on a steep natural hillside above the Calder Valley, where the people of Dewsbury, Batley and Birstall could look upon it and marvel at the wealth of its owner.

The Remains of Howley Hall

The hall was built by Sir John Savile in the late 1580s. Savile, a politician and magistrate, was Leeds' first mayor and was an influential figure in the court of King James I, but his son Thomas, who inherited the estate on Sir John's death in 1630, was a wavering royal supporter. Charles I nevertheless made him the first Earl of Sussex in 1642, shortly after which a relative, Sir John Savile of Lupset, took possession of the hall on behalf of the Parliamentarians.

In 1643 Parliamentarian generals met there to plan an attack on Wakefield, which took place successfully on 16 May. In response, a month later, the northern Royalist commander the Earl of Newcastle left Wakefield at the head of an army of 10,000 troops to attack Parliamentarian Bradford. On route, to prevent the Howley garrison launching a rearguard action, they laid siege to the hall, which somehow survived relatively unscathed. The Royalist army was met by between 3,000 and 4,000 men under General Ferdinando Fairfax, who unsuccessfully attempted to head-off the attack on the ill-prepared city. The confrontation became known as the Battle of Adwalton Moor. It was expected that the city's inhabitants would be slaughtered for their Parliamentarian sympathies but legend claims that a ghost appeared to the Earl of Newcastle and told him 'Pity poor Bradford'.

Thomas Savile subsequently defected to the Royalist cause and the family continued to live at Howley Hall until the hall went into decline and the stone was taken by locals for other buildings; in 1719 some of its masonry was used in the construction of Bradford's Old Presbyterian Chapel. What was left was demolished by gunpowder in 1730, to avoid further costly maintenance.

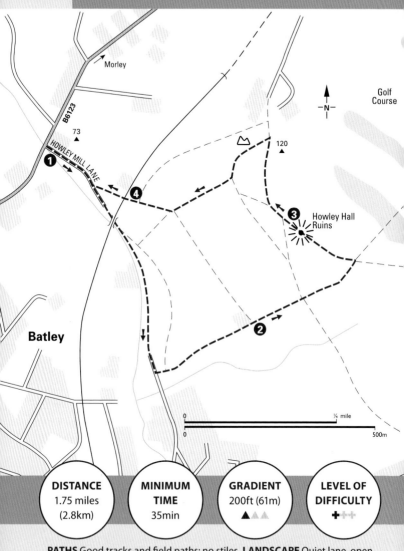

DISTANCE	MINIMUM TIME	GRADIENT	LEVEL OF DIFFICULTY
1.75 miles (2.8km)	35min	200ft (61m) ▲▲▲	✚✚✚

PATHS Good tracks and field paths; no stiles **LANDSCAPE** Quiet lane, open grassland **SUGGESTED MAP** OS Explorer 288 Bradford & Huddersfield
START/FINISH Grid reference: SE 247253 **DOG FRIENDLINESS** Dogs should be on lead until you reach open country. Be aware of horses and riders on the tracks
PARKING Park with care at the roadside, junction of Scotchman Lane/Timothy Lane and Howley Mill Lane, Batley. Do not park in Howley Mill Lane
PUBLIC TOILETS None on route **NOTE** Take special care when crossing the railway near the end of the walk

WALK 10 DIRECTIONS

❶ Take the public bridleway along Howley Mill Lane. Just 76yds (70m) after passing beneath the railway, the bridleway bears off the track to the left, along a tree- and shrub-lined path. Where it meets a surfaced track on a bend, bear left up the lane to walk past Howley Park Farm and through a gate beyond into a field.

❷ Maintain direction, staying with the ascending track when it bears right beneath electricity cables. Ignore tracks off to the left until, 240yds (219m) beyond the power lines, a wide grassy track cuts across your path. Turn left on this, past the skeletal ruins of Howley Hall; though little remains above ground, gaping holes hint at buried cellars concealing potential dangers for the curious. It is easy, however, to see why Sir John Savile chose this spot to build his

residence – the view is extensive, taking in Emley Moor TV transmitter, Castle Hill at Almondbury, the Peak District hills above Marsden and even parts of the South Pennines above the Calder Valley.

❸ Continue along the track, then bear left at a fork, dropping into scrub oak woodlands. Ignore the next left fork and keep ahead. The path rides the crest of an embankment then turns left, steeply downhill, to follow a wide and worn track down to a five-way junction of paths. Bear ahead-right here, descending gently towards a railway cottage.

❹ Pass through the gate and then cross the railway here with great care – trains climbing the gradient from the left are generally slower but those from the right travel at speed – to pass through the gate on the opposite side. Turn left, to descend the driveway back to Howley Mill Lane, there turning right back to the start.

⚘ IN THE AREA

The Battle of Adwalton Moor took place in what is now green belt land close to the heart of semi-rural Drighlington. It is the only recognised battleground in the Bradford district and several plaques have been erected to interpret the site for visitors. Bolling Hall Museum in Bradford also has a display about the battle.

🍴 EATING AND DRINKING

Years ago the Needless Inn, in Scotchman Lane, was almost called the Cardigan Arms, until someone pointed out that a pub nearby bore the same name; having two seemed needless. Open every day except Monday, it is popular with local walkers and their families, offering a children's menu and catering for pets outside on a decking area. It serves four cask ales and occasional guest beers. Look out for an illustration of Howley Hall displayed on the wall.

A TALE OF TWO BECKS

A little rural oasis between Leeds and Bradford.

This walk takes you through two delightful valleys: Fulneck Valley and Cockers Dale. In these wooded dells, criss-crossed by ancient packhorse tracks and hollow ways, you feel a long way from the surrounding cities.

On an attractive ridge between these valleys is the village of Tong, which dates back to before the Norman Conquest. Archaeological investigations of the foundations of the 12th-century chapel that predated its current church found traces of an even earlier structure. A grave marker found at the same time suggests that burials were taking place here before the Conquest.

An Ancient Route

Much of the area around Tong is green belt, and the village itself is a conservation area, with little new development having taken place since the 18th century. Ancient packhorse routes leave the village in every direction, and form the catalyst for many fine walks.

Keeper Lane, the ancient route along which this walk begins, crosses Pudsey Beck to head north to the village of Fulneck, where a community of non-conformist Moravians settled in the 18th century. Pre-Reformation dissenters from the Roman Catholic Church, the Moravians originated in Bohemia in the 15th century and spread to Moravia, both regions in the modern day Czech Republic. During the 18th century, their missionaries travelled overseas. One such group arrived in England on its way to America and was encouraged to settle in Yorkshire by a Church of England clergyman, Benjamin Ingham.

He gave them a 22-acre (9ha) estate for their settlement, which they named Fulneck, commemorating a town of that name in Moravia. The site sits high on a ridge with a splendid view across valley to Tong. The Moravians constructed a street along the ridge, and built a collection of handsome buildings along it, including a chapel, communal houses, family houses, a shop, inn, bakery and workshops. The hard-working, close-knit, self-sufficient community made a great impression on preacher John Wesley when he visited the area in 1780.

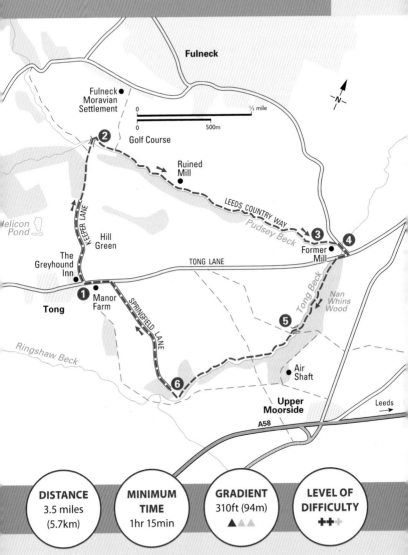

Fulneck

Fulneck
Moravian
Settlement

0
0   500m
½ mile

Golf Course

Ruined
Mill

LEEDS COUNTRY WAY

Pudsey Beck

❷

Hill
Green

KEEPER LANE

elicon
Pond

The
Greyhound
Inn

❶

Manor
Farm

Tong

Ringshaw Beck

SPRINGFIELD LANE

TONG LANE

Former
Mill

❸ ❹

Tong Beck

Nan
Whins
Wood

❺

Air
Shaft

❻

Upper
Moorside

A58

Leeds

N

DISTANCE	MINIMUM TIME	GRADIENT	LEVEL OF DIFFICULTY
3.5 miles (5.7km)	1hr 15min	310ft (94m) ▲▲▲	➕➕➕

PATHS Ancient causeways, hollow ways and field paths; 6 stiles

LANDSCAPE Mostly wooded valleys

SUGGESTED MAP OS Explorer 288 Bradford & Huddersfield

START/FINISH Grid reference: SE 222306

DOG FRIENDLINESS Can be off lead for most of walk

PARKING Lay-by in Tong village, near the village hall, or on the edge of village

PUBLIC TOILETS None on route

WALK 11 DIRECTIONS

❶ From Tong village walk up Keeper Lane which, after 265yds (242m), passes through a gate in a bend and becomes a sandy track. Walk steadily downhill, following a line of old causey stones, into woodland. Cross Pudsey Beck on a steel footbridge.

❷ Bear right off the bridge on the Leeds Country Way, following Pudsey Beck downstream along the edge of a golf course. The path leaves the course over a wooden step stile to pass through several fields and patches of scrubland, via a succession of stiles, dog-legging left and right but generally straightening the course set by the squiggling beck.

❸ Beyond pools full of small trout, the route passes through a kissing gate to briefly hug the stream, then crosses one final field to enter a fenced streamside path, beyond which a walled path brings you into a lane.

❹ Go right, past a converted mill, to a T-junction. Cross the main road and take a waymarked footpath between gateposts into Sykes' Wood.

> **🍴 EATING AND DRINKING**
>
> The Greyhound pub in Tong is used to welcoming walkers, with a full menu, including children's options, and a range of five regular Yorkshire ales and one guest beer. The Grade II listed pub even has its own cricket pitch.

Immediately bear right, through a kissing gate signed 'Leeds Country Way'. Follow the path, soon following Tong Beck upstream. After walking about 0.5 miles (800m) through woodland, take a footbridge over the beck and bear left by the boundary up to a metal kissing gate.

❺ Follow a path along the edge of a field, then through woodland. Keep left when the path eventually forks up to a gate, passing through the first of a pair of successive latched metal gates. Ignore side paths and stay on this bank to a kissing gate.

❻ Through that, turn away from the river along rising Springfield Lane. When you meet a road, cross to the pavement and go left, back into Tong.

> **🐾 ON THE WALK**
>
> As you re-enter Tong village you pass Manor Farm, home of Goodall's fresh dairy ice cream, made on site with milk from the family herd. Visitors to the Mistal café – which serves morning coffees, afternoon teas, snacks, and of course ice cream – can watch the milking and ice cream making processes. Youngsters will love meeting the farm's menagerie, which includes pot-bellied pigs, miniature Dexter cattle, pygmy goats and more.

SURPRISES ON THE CHEVIN

Enjoy woodland walks and panoramic
views across the Wharfe Valley.

This walk begins at Surprise View where, by strolling just a few paces from
your car, you can enjoy a breathtaking panorama across Otley and Lower
Wharfedale. Almscliffe Crag is a prominent landmark in the valley. On a clear
day, you might be able to see Simon's Seat, and even the famous White Horse
carved into the hillside at Kilburn.

The Chevin has traditionally been a popular destination for walkers and
picnickers. In 1944 Major Fawkes of Farnley Hall gave a piece of land on the
Chevin to the people of Otley. By 1989, when it was designated a local nature
reserve, Chevin Forest Park had grown to 700 acres (283ha) of woodland,
heath and gritstone crags. The park is criss-crossed by many good waymarked
paths and local people come here to walk their dogs, while the broad forest
tracks are ideal for horse riders and mountain bikers.

A Market Town on the River

Immediately below the Chevin is the market town of Otley, straddling the
River Wharfe, and well worth visiting in its own right. Wharfemeadows
Park offers riverside strolls, gardens and a children's play area. Thomas
Chippendale, the famous furniture maker, was born in Otley in 1710.

Otley was granted its market charter back in 1222, and the cobbled market
square still occupies the centre of town. On market days (Tuesdays, Fridays
and Saturdays) the stalls overflow along the main street of Kirkgate. There are
weekly livestock markets, too, and Otley Show, each spring, is a big date in
the local calendar. The Otley Folk Festival attracts music lovers every autumn;
over a long weekend you can hardly move for mummers and morris dancers.
Otley is famous – or perhaps infamous – for having more pubs per head of
population than anywhere else in Yorkshire. Even though a by-pass now
keeps a lot of traffic away, it's still a busy little town.

As you wander the trails around the Chevin, bear in mind that you're in
good company. Sherpa Tenzing Norgay, with Sir Edmund Hillary one of the
two people to first climb Everest, scaled Otley Chevin on 2 June, 1977, when
visiting the town for a book signing.

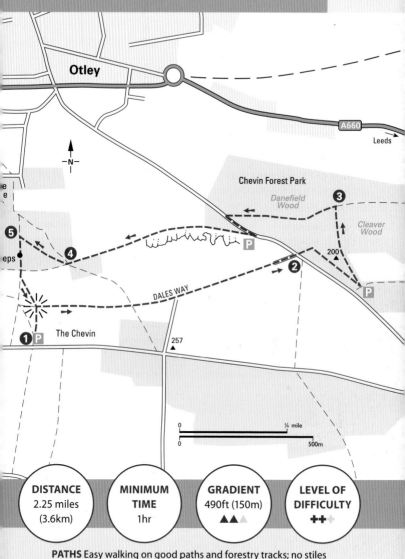

DISTANCE
2.25 miles
(3.6km)

MINIMUM TIME
1hr

GRADIENT
490ft (150m)
▲▲▲

LEVEL OF DIFFICULTY
+++

PATHS Easy walking on good paths and forestry tracks; no stiles
LANDSCAPE Heath and woodland **SUGGESTED MAP** OS Explorer 297 Lower
Wharfedale & Washburn Valley **START/FINISH** Grid reference: SE 204441
DOG FRIENDLINESS Dogs can run free across the Chevin but take care on roads
PARKING Free car park at Beacon House near The Royalty Inn, York Gate, Otley
PUBLIC TOILETS At the White House Café, on route **NOTE** The flight of steps
at the end, between the White House Café and the car park, comes as
a sting in the tail!

Opposite: Chevin Forest Park is rich in woodland trails

WALK 12 DIRECTIONS

❶ From the far end of the car park you have access to the Chevin Ridge, with its splendid bird's-eye view of Otley and Lower Wharfedale. Follow the ridge path, a section of the Dales Way, to the right, keeping to the higher branch where it shortly splits. Beyond a gate, keep ahead at a junction and descend on a track to meet a road beside Danefield House.

❷ Cross the road carefully and take the bridleway opposite, which swings right, into woodland, to parallel the road. At a trail junction by a car park double back sharp left, descending into Cleaver Wood on a signed permissive bridlepath. While walking you might spot the most spectacular – and recent – resident of the woodland, the red kite. The last few paces zig-zag down to meet a track at a T-junction.

❸ Bear left, through Danefield Wood, back to the road. Turnm left up the pavement here for 88yds (80m) then cross into the car park on the opposite side. Pass by a carved boulder into a lane which climbs from the car park, past the rocky outcrops of the former East Chevin Quarry. As the track levels it offers fine views across the town of Otley. Ignore any side trails until, 0.6 miles (1km) beyond the car park, you reach a T-junction with a trail that slopes across your track.

❹ Bear right here for 110yds (100m), to a point at which a flight of steps rising to your left is encountered. Just beyond this junction is the White House Café, which is a good place to stop for refreshments.

❺ The final stage is, of course, the ascent of those steps, more than 200 of them, which lead unrelentingly to a tree-line track. Cross that track and continue the ascent up a grassy slope, forking left near the top to ease the gradient slightly and return to Beacon House car park.

✿ IN THE AREA

Visit Otley, the characterful little market town by the River Wharfe. The little nooks and corners are well worth investigating. In the churchyard you will find an elaborate memorial to the 23 workers who were killed during the construction of the nearby Bramhope railway tunnel between 1845 and 1849.

🍴 EATING AND DRINKING

The White House Café, tucked away in the heart of the woodland, comes as a welcome surprise near the end of the walk. The café is run by Leeds City Council's Adult Social Care Department and offers a delicious selection of simple snacks, from sandwiches and toasties to soup and jacket potatoes. Dogs and muddy boots are both welcome.

SOURCE OF
THE DEARNE

An expedition to the West Yorkshire source
of one of South Yorkshire's rivers.

The River Dearne is held by most to belong to South Yorkshire. In the
course of its 19-mile (30km) journey to its confluence with the River Don at
Conisbrough, then ultimately into the North Sea at Goole as the River Ouse, it
flows through such South Yorkshire towns as Wath upon Dearne, Bolton upon
Deane and Adwick upon Dearne. Yet the river has some of its finest moments
in West Yorkshire, and indeed has its source in that county.

Through Ancient Woodland to the Source

Stephen Wood, the first woodland encountered, was once owned by the
Wentworths of Bretton Hall, as were others in the area. Some 6.25miles (10km)
east of its source on Birdsedge, near Upper Cumberworth, the Dearne flows
through the Bretton Estate, now home to the Yorkshire Sculpture Park. Later
woodland owners included the Bosvilles of Gunthwaite, and 19th-century mill
owner Walter Norton of Rockwood House, who also created the pond passed
on this walk. Many of the sycamore and beech trees in the woods were
probably planted to be used as rollers in textile mills, though with the decline
of the British industry they have been allowed to flourish.

The woods, now owned by a building products company, are looked
after by Upper Dearne Woodlands Conservation Group, and are a haven for
wildlife. Among the bird species seen here are tawny owl, flycatcher, tree
creeper and the goldcrest, Britain's smallest songbird. Large colonies of hairy
northern wood ant make their homes in large nests on the woodland floor,
while the grey squirrel is a common sight, running up tree trunks and along
branches. The variety of wildlife habitat has been significantly improved by
the conservation group's restoration of the pond.

Among the flowers that add colour through spring and summer are pink
purslane, yellow saxifrage and red campion.

The source of the Dearne lies in a spring, in a field above the hamlet of
Birdsedge. Many mills were powered by the river along its length; Birdsedge
Mill, built in the 18th century less than a mile (1.6km) from the source, is the
highest and its pond is as close to the source as the walk is able to go.

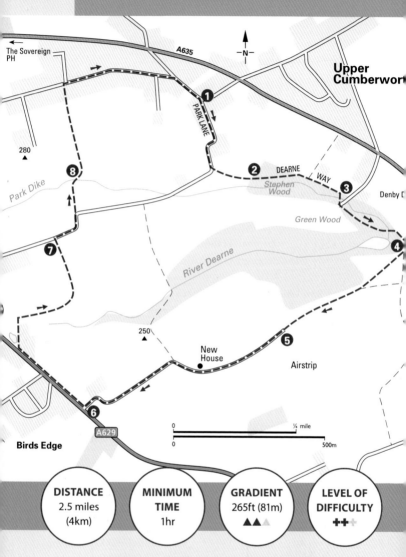

The Sovereign
PH

A635

Upper
Cumberwort

PARK LANE

280 ▲

1

Park Dike

8

2 DEARNE WAY

Stephen
Wood

3

Denby D

Green Wood

7

4

River Dearne

250 ▲

New
House

5

Airstrip

6

A629

Birds Edge

0 — ¼ mile
0 — 500m

DISTANCE	MINIMUM TIME	GRADIENT	LEVEL OF DIFFICULTY
2.5 miles (4km)	1hr	▲▲▲ 265ft (81m)	╋╋╋

PATHS Good field and woodland paths; 6 stiles
LANDSCAPE Pastoral countryside with wooded stream and millponds
SUGGESTED MAP OS Explorer 288 Bradford & Huddersfield
START/FINISH Junction of Hill Road and Park Lane, Upper Cumberworth;
Grid reference: SE 207086 **DOG FRIENDLINESS** Dogs can run freely in the
woodlands but should be on lead in fields and roads
PARKING Park considerately in nearby streets **PUBLIC TOILETS** None on route

Upper Cumberworth

WALK 13 DIRECTIONS

1 Walk down Park Lane and, at the second of two barns, turn right, then left. Within a few paces the lane turns right again but here take a path on the left, descending steps through the wall and a gate. Follow the fence on your left along a field-edge, toward woodland. Go through a second gate and over a stile into Stephen Wood.

2 Bear left, along the Dearne Way (marked by a miner's lamp), at a fork by an information board. At the first junction bear right, staying with the Dearne Way, ignoring a path up to your left. When you see a footbridge below to your right, descend the bank and cross a Dearne Way-marked stile in a fence – don't cross the footbridge.

3 Cross another footbridge ahead, over Park Dike, and go through a narrow gap between wooden posts into Green Wood, past an information board. Ignore paths off to your right, and stay ahead. Bear left at a third board, away from a pond on your right, to reach a step stile in around 40 paces. Cross this and turn right into a fenced lane, still on the Dearne Way, for 90yds (82m). Take the path on the right, over a footbridge and up steps to a stile.

4 Three options present themselves here: yours heads right, diagonally across a field towards the walled corner of a wood. There, pass through a gap to the right of a gate and keep ahead, along a faint track that parallels an airstrip over the wall on your left.

5 Pass through a gap on the side of the next metal field gate, into a walled lane, which curves right, around New House. Keep to the track that now bends left, ignoring a path to the right, past Birds Edge Farmhouse to the road.

6 On the road, turn right. After 330yds (302m), just beyond a bus shelter and half-way along a patch of off-road residents' parking, take a path to the right, descending past Birds Edge Mill and its old millpond. After crossing the pond's outflow, turn right, ascending among trees to cross a stile into a field. Stay on the right fenced edge, once again following Dearne Way markers, into an enclosed path by a field.

7 At the end, pass through a gap on the left of a gate into a walled lane. Turn right. The lane kinks left then right, leave it here on a signed field path that continues ahead, over a stile and through a gate. Descend the field ahead, with the wall on your left, to stepping stones over Park Dike.

8 Ascend the opposite bank, bearing right, and climb the field against the right wall, to pass through a gate and gap at the top. Follow the right edge of the next field, under power lines, to a wide, 35yd-long (32m) field entrance, into Carr House Lane. Turn right, downhill, back into the village.

JOURNEY THROUGH AN OLD MILL TOWN

A speedy flight from a bustling town centre whisks you into peaceful countryside.

Cleckheaton is a small, bustling town on the River Spen, with a commercial heart as yet undepleted by out-of-town shopping centres. Clustered around the junction of the A643 Huddersfield/Morley and A638 Wakefield/Bradford roads, it feels as though it should be busier than it is. The M62, however, has relieved the town of much of its choking traffic, and though the town was once served by two lines, and had two stations, it no longer has a railway. Life in Cleckheaton then, is allowed to progress at a far more affable pace.

It takes surprisingly little time to escape the centre and find yourself surrounded by greenery. Directly to the east of the town centre lie open fields, angling lakes and woodland, and a good network of paths that transport you into the countryside within minutes.

Once a thriving textile town, Cleckheaton specialised in carding, the process by which clumps of raw materials such as wool or cotton are combed into straight fibres, ready to be spun. By 1838 there were at least 11 carding mills in and around Cleckheaton and 50 years later its output won it an undisputed reputation as the carding capital of the world.

The Price of Success

Cleckheaton's mills, like many others in the years of the Industrial Revolution, employed children on starvation wages to insert the staples into leather for carding the wool. And there were those who resented the mechanisation processes introduced in the early 19th century. In April 1812, local croppers made redundant by cloth-finishing machines attacked Rawfolds Mill with the aim of destroying the equipment; two were mortally wounded. A week later, the owner of another mill in the town was murdered. More than 100 suspects were rounded up and 64 were charged. Three were executed for the murder and 14 were hung for the attack on Rawfolds Mill. It was one of the worst incidents involving the Luddites, a country-wide working class movement that protested against increasing mechanisation by destroying machinery. They took their name from the mythical figure Ned Ludd, or Captain Ludd, who according to folklore was first to smash equipment, in a fit of rage.

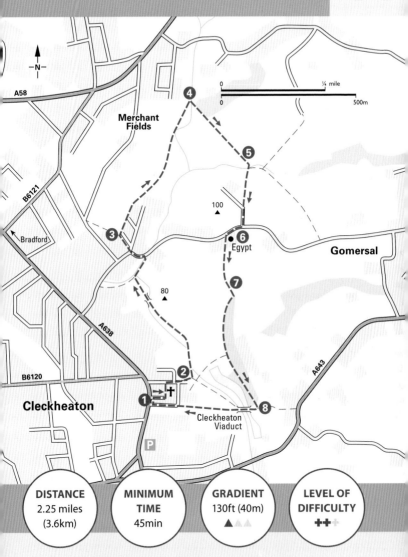

A58

Merchant
Fields

B6121

Bradford

④

⑤

100 ▲

③

⑥
Egypt

Gomersal

A638

80 ▲

⑦

B6120

Cleckheaton

②

①

⑧

A643

Cleckheaton
Viaduct

P

DISTANCE	MINIMUM TIME	GRADIENT	LEVEL OF DIFFICULTY
2.25 miles (3.6km)	45min	130ft (40m) ▲▲▲	++

PATHS Generally good field paths and tracks; 11 stiles

LANDSCAPE Wetland, farmland and urban fringe

SUGGESTED MAP OS Explorer 288 Bradford & Huddersfield

START/FINISH Grid reference: SE 191253

DOG FRIENDLINESS Dogs can exercise freely but should be on lead through farms and around livestock **PARKING** Free short-stay (4hr) parking in the town centre **PUBLIC TOILETS** In Cleckheaton

Walk
14
Cleckheaton

WALK 14 DIRECTIONS

❶ Along Chapel Street, immediately jink left into a back street behind the Independent Methodist Church. Cross the road at the bottom and take the track opposite, which descends to cross a stream into a field. Bear left here, to the corner of a pond.

❷ Bear left on boardwalk over a meadow. The boardwalk ends at a gap stile through a fence, the path continuing along the field-edge and through a kissing gate. After crossing a footbridge, a flag path bears you to a junction. Turn right, along a streamside path to a road, met on an S-bend. Turn left, cross carefully on the bend and take the signed snicket between Brookfield View and Kestrel View.

❸ This brings you to a step stile into a field. Turn right, keeping close to the field-edge and ignoring any gaps or stiles offering access into housing on your right. The path leaves housing behind when it passes through a gap to be guided below paddocks. Cross a step stile and continue along the right-hand edge of the field beyond, on what soon becomes an obvious worn path paralleling a stream.

❹ In the far corner, cross a bridge over the stream and follow the fence on your right to a step stile. Ascend the next field, with the fence now on your left, bearing gently right to follow the hedge along the top edge. Half-way along the hedge, step through a stile to continue in the same direction along the opposite side. It guides you to a gap stile by a field gate in the corner.

❺ Through this, bear ahead, across the field, to cross a stream and, a few paces beyond, a step stile over a fence. Head across the next field, to its top-right corner (to be sure, aim for the left-most of two phone line poles ahead). On meeting a farm track in the top-right corner of the field, turn left to the road.

❻ Cross to the pavement and turn right, toward Egypt. At the far end of the first building passed on your left, turn left and mount an iron step stile into the yard of Egypt Farm. Pass through the yard, crossing a stile by the field gate opposite and keeping ahead down the field beyond, with the fence on your right, to the far corner, where a gap stile lets you into the field below.

❼ The fence on your left guides you down to another stile, beyond which the route runs between a fence and a wooded embankment. Where the fence turns right, keep ahead on a firm path which gently climbs to a junction.

❽ Through the wooden bollards turn right to cross lofty Cleckheaton Viaduct, which offers fine views across Cleckheaton and the Spen Valley as it passes above Harry Mann Dam. Keep ahead beyond the bridge, up a wide track leading back to Bradford Road.

UNDERCLIFFE'S GLORIOUS TRIBUTE TO THE DEAD

Even in death the Victorians believed they should be looked up to. In a hillside cemetery in Bradford, they got just that.

Undercliffe Cemetery is unlike any other. Here, gathered within the 25-acre (10ha) grounds of a former mansion, are obelisks, Egyptian tombs, Celtic crosses and mausoleums that wouldn't look too out of place in Vatican City.

The Bradford Cemetery Company began interring people at Undercliffe in 1854. A notice in the *Bradford Guardian* at the time, declared that 'the views of the surrounding country from various portions of the ground are not to be surpassed in the neighbourhood of Bradford', was no exaggeration. Stand by the Smith Monument at the western end of the cemetery and the city is spread out at your feet, and with views extending north to Baildon Moor and west to Ovenden Moor, above Halifax.

Location, Location, Location

Burial prices within Undercliffe Cemetery depended on location. The most expensive spots lined a grand promenade running east to west. Among the great and the good buried there are Robert Milligan, merchant and first mayor of Bradford; Sir Jacob Behrens, another successful merchant; and architect William Mawson, who designed some of Bradford's most important buildings, including City Hall and the Wool Exchange.

One of the joys of exploring Undercliffe, however, is finding the memorials, not only to those great and good, but to the city's tradesmen such as plumbers, saddlers and ironmongers; to soldiers who fell at battlegrounds such as Ypres; to the puppeteer, the surgeon, the theatre manager and the fishmonger's wife. Or poor Fred Greenwood Smith, who died in a tram accident in Girlington in 1889.

After the site was threatened by development in the 1980s it was taken into the care of the Undercliffe Cemetery Charity, which carries out conservation work, runs education programmes and produces guides and newsletters. The cemetery, which holds the remains of more than 123,500 Bradfordians in more than 23,000 graves, still accepts burials today. Whether you go there to admire the monuments or simply to take exercise, you'll be that bit closer to heaven in this spiritually uplifting place.

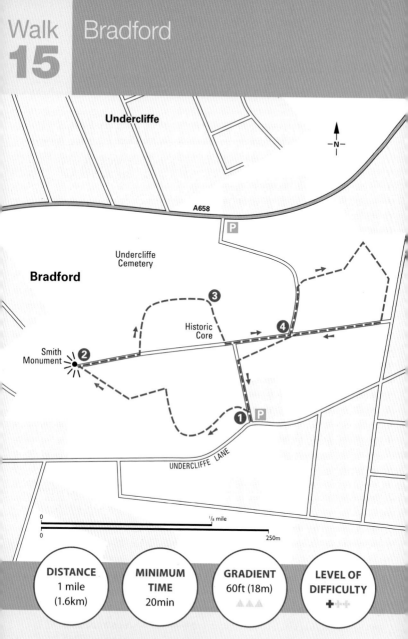

Uncliffe

A658

Undercliffe
Cemetery

Bradford

3

Historic
Core

4

Smith
Monument **2**

1

UNDERCLIFFE LANE

0   ¹/₈ mile
0   250m

DISTANCE	MINIMUM TIME	GRADIENT	LEVEL OF DIFFICULTY
1 mile (1.6km)	20min	60ft (18m)	

PATHS Surfaced tracks and well-maintained grassy paths; no stiles
LANDSCAPE Cemetery paths **SUGGESTED MAP** OS Explorer 288 Bradford &
Huddersfield **START/FINISH** Main entrance, Undercliffe Cemetery; Grid reference:
SE 174341 **DOG FRIENDLINESS** Dogs should be under control at all times and
mess removed **PARKING** Car parks in Undercliffe Lane and Otley Road; on-street
parking near by **PUBLIC TOILETS** None on route **NOTE** Car parks close at 8.30pm
April to September and 4.30pm October to March

WALK 15 DIRECTIONS

❶ From the gatehouse, turn left on to a grassy path. Swing right in front of the tribute to surgeon Thomas Beaumont, then left, by the monument to John Robertshaw, along a grassy path. Keep ahead, past a mound bearing a small yew, then bear right along the perimeter path and mount steps to the towering Smith monument. The view from here goes some way to explaining its attraction as a burial place for the city's most prominent citizens. Just as you can see across the entire city of Bradford, away to the moors of Ovenden and Baildon, so the populations of those places could look to the resting places of those who regarded themselves as Bradford's leading lights.

❷ Head down the main drive from here for 110yds (100m), then bear left, between the Gurney and Feather monuments, down to a grassy crossroads. Turn right, past Private George Young, and bear right at a fork, to some steps.

❸ Climb these and keep ahead into what is referred to as the historic core. Here you'll find some of the most impressive monuments, tombs and mausoleums in the entire cemetery. Climb the steps out of the historic core and turn left along the main promenade.

❹ Bear left at a fork, along a surfaced track. After just 33yds (30m) bear right, on a grassy track past the memorial to puppet theatre proprietor Walter Calver, who performed for Queen Victoria. Encountering the perimeter path again, turn right back to the main promenade. Follow this for 185yds (170m) – past a splendid monument to the memory of a Bradford fishmonger's wife – to turn left on to another surfaced track, back to the start.

> 🍽 **EATING AND DRINKING**
>
> When in Bradford, the only dish to eat is curry. The city has dozens, if not hundreds of curry houses. One of the finest – and one offering great value – is the Karachi, established in Neal Street for decades. You take it as you find it – most diners eat with their hands, stuffing the delicious food into their mouths with chapattis – but none other than television chef Rick Stein is a fan, and who are we to argue?

> 🐾 **ON THE WALK**
>
> The Illingworth Mausoleum, in the area referred to as the historical core, is one of the cemetery's highlights. This monument to the memory of Bradford liberal politician Alfred Illingworth was designed in the form of an Egyptian temple, bearing the insignia of the sun god Ra. It is guarded by a pair of granite sphinxes and originally had huge bronze doors.

RAILWAYS ABOVE THE HOLME VALLEY

Gentle pastures and wide-open views before crossing the Penistone Line

In the mid-1800s the North's industrial might couldn't grow fast enough and the waterways were beginning to be regarded as too slow, and so railway mania took hold.

The Huddersfield and Sheffield Junction Railway was formed to connect those two cities by rail. From the start, though, the company faced severe difficulties. The route had to be bored beneath hills, several rivers had to be bridged, and great cuttings had to be dug and embankments raised.

Work on the line began in 1845, but the company was quickly absorbed by the Manchester and Leeds Railway, which in turn became the Lancashire and Yorkshire Railway. Costs soared, as Parliament refused to allow the line to meet the Manchester route in a tunnel just outside Huddersfield, on grounds of safety, resulting in expensive and timely engineering work.

A Difficult Start and a New Lease of Life

The line eventually opened on 1 July, 1850, but to the railway company's embarrassment the inaugural train stalled in Thurstonland Tunnel, between Brockholes and Stocksmoor stations. Half the coaches had to be uncoupled. The engine took the front carriages to Stocksmoor Station, while the others remained in the 1,631-yard (1,491m) tunnel, awaiting rescue. Wet rails, with which the underpowered locomotive engine couldn't cope, were blamed – possibly the first recorded case of 'wrong kind of water on the line'.

Future years saw major problems: Denby Dale's viaduct, built of timber, collapsed twice before someone thought of rebuilding it in stone. Penistone's stone viaduct collapsed in 1916, though the driver and fireman of the loco crossing it at the time survived by leaping from the footplate.

The Beeching cuts of the early 1960s threatened the line with closure but the Transport Minister Barbara Castle rejected the idea. In more recent years the line has been given a new lease of life with the creation of a new halt to serve Meadowhall, the shopping complex near Sheffield. The line's role as a community asset is also promoted by the Penistone Line Partnership – music and real ale trains are a regular attraction.

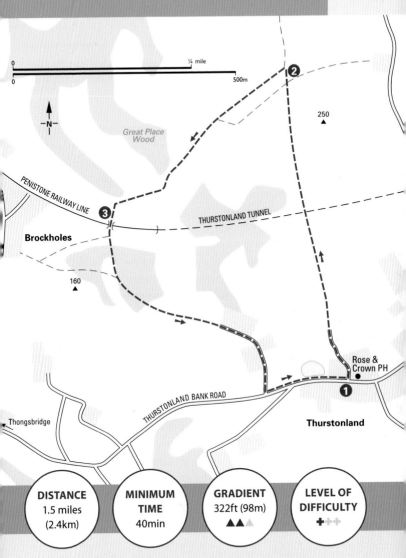

0 — ¼ mile
0 — 500m

—N—

Great Place Wood

250 ▲

PENISTONE RAILWAY LINE

❸

THURSTONLAND TUNNEL

Brockholes

160 ▲

Rose & Crown PH ●

❶

THURSTONLAND BANK ROAD

← Thongsbridge

Thurstonland

DISTANCE	MINIMUM TIME	GRADIENT	LEVEL OF DIFFICULTY
1.5 miles (2.4km)	40min	322ft (98m) ▲▲▲	✛✛✛

PATHS Good field paths and tracks, a little mud; 5 stiles

LANDSCAPE Pastoral countryside, with one climb

SUGGESTED MAP OS Explorer 288 Bradford & Huddersfield

START/FINISH Rose and Crown pub, Thurstonland; Grid reference: SE 164104

DOG FRIENDLINESS Free to exercise unless livestock is grazing

PARKING Roadside parking in the village – please be considerate to residents

PUBLIC TOILETS None on route

Walk 16 Thurstonland

WALK 16 DIRECTIONS

❶ Take the signed footpath next door-but-one to the left of the Rose and Crown pub, past The Barn, Upperfold. The obvious green lane beyond immediately offers views across the Holme Valley on your left and soon, on your right, across the valley of Shepley Dike, to Emley Moor telecommunications and TV transmitter mast, the highest free-standing structure in the UK. Cross a tricky stone stile into the field ahead, through which a less-pronounced path follows the wall on your left, to a stone gap stile. Keep ahead, the wall now on your right, to cross another stile beyond which the path continues diagonally ahead-right over the subsequent field, to meet and follow a wall on your right. Where this bears off, continue ahead and across to a stone gatepost.

❷ Although the right of way turns left here to follow the wall downhill, the easier, more frequented option is to cross the wooden step stile to the right of the collapsed gate ahead and turn left down a well-worn grassy path, which becomes a lane passing through Great Place Wood, then cuts diagonally across the next field to its far corner.

❸ Here a bridge carries you over the Penistone railway line, near Thurstonland Tunnel, scene of the 1850 humiliation. Beyond, take the continuing path, ignoring stiles on your right, up to a kissing gate in the top right-hand corner of the wood. Continue ahead up a well-worn path by a shallow wooded clough, to a stone stile. The walled lane beyond leads to a surfaced driveway. Carry on up this, trending right past cottages and farmhouses known as Top of the Hill, back to Thurstonland Bank Road. Turn left, along the pavement, back to the village.

☕ IN THE AREA

Just a short train ride away from nearby Brockholes is Huddersfield's wonderful Grade I listed railway station, described by poet and heritage champion John Betjeman as 'one of the best early railway stations in England'. It was designed by the architect James Piggot Pritchett and built between 1845 and 1850, with a classical-style facade incorporating eight huge Corinthian columns.

🍴 EATING AND DRINKING

After climbing back from the railway line you'll be ready for some refreshment, and the friendly Rose and Crown in Thurstonland serves fine beers – including award-winning ales from the independent West Yorkshire Brass Monkey Brewery – as well as fine home-made food. It welcomes families – there's a specific kids' menu – and well-behaved pets.

A TASTE OF ROMBALD'S MOOR

Sampling West Yorkshire moorland from the village of Burley in Wharfedale.

According to legend, a giant by the name of Rombald used to live in these parts. While striding across the moor (in some versions of the story he was being chased by his angry wife) he dislodged a stone from a gritstone outcrop, and thus created the Calf, of the Cow and Calf rocks.

Job Senior, the Hermit of Rombald's Moor

Another local character is celebrated a public house called The Hermit at Burley Woodhead. Job Senior worked as a farm labourer, before succumbing to the demon drink. He met an elderly widow, who lived at Coldstream Beck, on the edge of Rombald's Moor. Thinking he might get his hands on her money and home, Job married the old crone. Though she died soon after, Job took no profit. The family of her first husband pulled the cottage down, in Job's absence, leaving him homeless and penniless once more.

Enraged, he built himself a tiny hovel from the ruins of the house. Here he lived in squalor on a diet of home-grown potatoes, which he roasted on a peat fire. He must have cut a strange figure, with a coat of multi-coloured patches and trousers held up with twine. He had long, lank hair, a matted beard and his legs were bandaged with straw. He made slow, rheumatic progress around Rombald's Moor with the aid of two crooked sticks.

His eccentric lifestyle soon had people flocking to see him. He offered weather predictions, and even advised visitors about their love lives. The possessor of a remarkable voice, he 'sang for his supper' as he lay on his bed of dried bracken and heather. These impromptu performances encouraged Job to sing in nearby villages, and even in the theatres of Leeds and Bradford. His speciality was sacred songs, which he would deliver with great feeling. Nevertheless, his unwashed appearance meant that accommodation was never forthcoming, forcing him to bed down in barns or outhouses.

It was while staying in a barn that he was struck down with cholera. He was taken to Carlton Workhouse, where he died in 1857, aged 77. A huge crowd of people gathered at his funeral. Job Senior, the hermit of Rombald's Moor, was buried in the churchyard of Burley in Wharfedale.

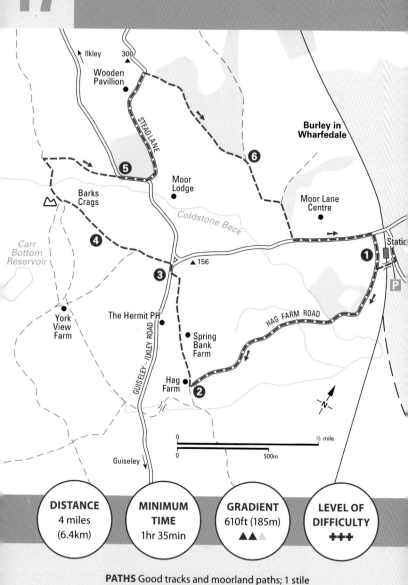

Ilkley
300
Wooden
Pavillion
STEAD LANE
Burley in
Wharfedale
5
Moor
Lodge
6
Barks
Crags
Coldstone Beck
Moor Lane
Centre
Carr
Bottom
Reservoir
4
156
3
Static
1
P
York
View
Farm
The Hermit PH
GUISELEY - ILKLEY ROAD
Spring
Bank
Farm
HAG FARM ROAD
Hag
Farm
2
N
0   ½ mile
0   500m
Guiseley

DISTANCE	MINIMUM TIME	GRADIENT	LEVEL OF DIFFICULTY
4 miles (6.4km)	1hr 35min	610ft (185m) ▲▲△	+++

PATHS Good tracks and moorland paths; 1 stile
LANDSCAPE Moor and arable land
SUGGESTED MAP OS Explorer 297 Lower Wharfedale & Washburn Valley
START/FINISH Grid reference: SE 163458
DOG FRIENDLINESS Dogs can be off lead unless sheep are grazing
PARKING Burley in Wharfedale Railway Station
PUBLIC TOILETS None on route

WALK 17 DIRECTIONS

❶ From the station car park, cross the line via a footbridge and go left along quiet Hag Farm Road, beyond the housing and between fields up to Hag Farm.

❷ There bear right, with the farm buildings on your left, through a wooden wicket gate into a field. Follow the wall on your left to the far corner, where a fenced path leads to a surfaced driveway. Across this, pass through a kissing gate to the left of Spring Bank Cottage, and keep ahead across the open field beyond to a stone gap stile. Cross two subsequent small fields before passing through a kissing gate into a driveway. Turn left, to the road.

❸ Cross to the pavement and turn right for 66yds (60m) to a Dales Way Link sign, which directs you through a small gate in a fence, along an obvious path through gorse on to Rombald's Moor. Where this forks after 220yds (201m), near an isolated house, keep right, along the moor edge, which offers views across Wharfedale.

❹ At the next clear fork, 570yds (521m) on, bear right again and keep ahead at the junction met immediately. The path soon joins with another from the left to cross Coldstone Beck. On the rare occasions when the beck is in spate, search a little further upstream for a drier crossing. As you climb away,

bear right and follow a path that descends to meet a road by a sharp bend.

❺ Walk 210yds (192m) down the road to another sharp bend. Take Stead Lane, which continues between fields beyond a couple of houses. As it swings left towards a farm, 130yds (119m) beyond a wooden pavilion, leave it by dropping to a dilapidated kissing gate on your right. Cross the field beyond with woodland to your left to another kissing gate. Follow the field boundary on your right to a third kissing gate and take the fenced path beyond.

> ### 🍴 EATING AND DRINKING
>
> The Hermit is a welcoming stone-built pub in Burley Woodhead, whose name recalls the eccentric local character described in the walk's introduction. During the walk it is easy to make a short detour to the inn, with its oak-panelled and beamed rooms and views of Wharfedale. Alternatively, the village of Burley in Wharfedale boasts a number of places to get a bite to eat.

❻ Turn right along the track met at the end, bearing off after 200yds (183m), along a fenced path leading to a second track within trees. Follow it right for 220yds (201m) to the road and go left. Return to the station by turning right along Hag Farm Road, just before a railway bridge.

VIEWS OF CASTLE HILL FROM FARNLEY TYAS

A delightful valley and views of Huddersfield's most prominent landmark.

As you gaze down into the Woodsome Valley from Farnley Tyas, you feel a long way from the mills and terraced houses that typify most of the county.

On this walk from Farnley Tyas, the tower on Castle Hill dominates your view. Village and hill face each other across the valley, and across the centuries. The village was mentioned in the Domesday Book, as 'Fereleia' but the history of Castle Hill extends at least 4,000 years. The site was inhabited by neolithic settlers who defended it with earth ramparts. Axe heads and other flint tools dating from this era and found here during archaeological digs are now displayed in Huddersfield's Tolson Museum. The Stone Age settlers were just the first of many peoples who saw the hill's defensive potential. Its exposed position, with uninterrupted views on all sides, made it an ideal place for a fortification.

Almost 900 years ago the de Lacy family built a motte-and-bailey castle on the site, having been given land as a reward for their part in the Norman Conquest. Though the structure was demolished in the 14th century, the mound has been known ever since as Castle Hill. Most of the earthworks and ramparts that can be seen today date from medieval times.

A Hill-top Village and the Royal Corkers

The name of Farnley Tyas, an attractive hill-top village, sounds rather posh for workaday West Yorkshire. Once plain Farnley, the village gained its double-barrelled moniker to differentiate it from other Farnleys – one near Leeds, the other near Otley. The 'Tyas' suffix is the name of the area's most prominent family, who owned land here from the 13th century onwards.

Originally a farm, the Golden Cock has been at the centre of village life since the 17th century. During the 19th century, a group called the Royal Corkers used to ride over from Huddersfield to enjoy supper at the Golden Cock. Corks were placed on the dining table, with the last person (usually the only person!) to pick up a cork having to pay for supper for the whole party. Any newcomer to the group would unknowingly pick up a cork – but none of the regulars ever did – thus leaving the newcomer to pick up the bill.

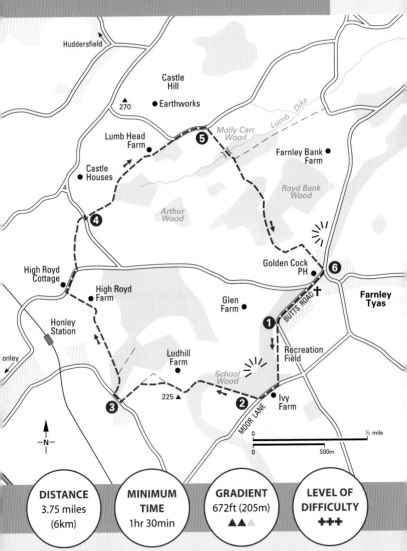

Huddersfield

Castle
Hill

● Earthworks
▲ 270

Lumb Dike

Molly Carr
Wood

5

Lumb Head
Farm

Farnley Bank ●
Farm

Castle
● Houses

Royd Bank
Wood

Arthur
Wood

4

High Royd
Cottage ●

High Royd
● Farm

Golden Cock
PH ●

6

Farnley
Tyas

Honley
Station

Glen
Farm ●

BUTTS ROAD

✝

onley ←

Ludhill
Farm ●

1

Recreation
Field

225 ▲

School
Wood

2

Ivy
Farm ●

3

—N—

MOOR LANE

0
0   500m   ½ mile

⬤ DISTANCE	⬤ MINIMUM TIME	⬤ GRADIENT	⬤ LEVEL OF DIFFICULTY
3.75 miles (6km)	1hr 30min	672ft (205m) ▲▲▲	+++

PATHS Field paths, a little road walking on quiet lanes; 14 stiles
LANDSCAPE Arable, rolling countryside and woodland
SUGGESTED MAP OS Explorer 288 Bradford & Huddersfield
START/FINISH Grid reference: SE 161124
DOG FRIENDLINESS Can be off lead but watch for traffic and livestock
PARKING Roadside parking by the recreation ground in Farnley Tyas
PUBLIC TOILETS None on route

WALK 18 DIRECTIONS

❶ Enter the recreation field and follow the wall to your right. Beyond a second field, follow a walled track out to meet a road. Go right (this is Moor Lane).

❷ About 100yds (91m) past Ivy Farm, turn right down a track. When the track bends right toward Ludhill Farm, drop left to a walled path. Walk downhill to take a stile by a gate, strike left across a field to a gap in the corner, and bear right, descending more steeply. The way then swings left to accompany a sunken path to meet a road.

❸ Go right, downhill, but just after cottages, turn right through a gate, on a track into woodland. After 50yds (46m) bear left on a lesser path descending to a stile. Cross a field (aim for the farm ahead), a stream then go up through woodland. Cross a field to the left of High Royd Farm, ahead. A path leads right, out to a drive, which climbs to meet a road opposite High Royd Cottage. Walk right for 100yds (91m). Where the road bears right, take a stile in the wall on your left. Follow an enclosed path to a stile and bear right, uphill, along the edge of a plantation. Through a rickety stile in a wall, head diagonally across a field. Follow the left-hand edge of the next field. The path levels out as you meet a road.

❹ Go right here, for 20yds (18m), turning left through a kissing gate. Head away on a field-edge path soon passing through a waymarked gap to continue, with the wall now on your right, toward a wood. Over a stile, keep to the right-hand edge of the next field. Leaving the wood behind and heading to Lumb Head Farm, with the wall now on your left, you can see Emley Moor mast far to your right. Cross a stile then a field and a step stile. Wind right, through a farmyard, and join the access track to meet a road. Go right here, down Lumb Lane. After a couple of cottages, pass through a gap stile in a wall on the right.

❺ Walk into the valley, following the wall, then the fence. Take a stile to cross Lumb Dike. Ascend the opposite bank to an old stile and keep ahead, through woodland, to a stile with dog gate. Follow the right-hand field-edge to the far corner. Pass through a gap in the wall and enter woodland, crossing a footbridge. The path leaves the woodland briefly, re-entering through a wall gap. Follow the path to cross a stream within a few paces then veering right to rise beside a stream valley. The path emerges from the woodland to pass through two stiles into a field. Ascend its left edge and, at the next wall, where the stream vanishes, turn left into a lane, which goes through a kissing gate and ascends to the road.

❻ Turn right into the village. At the Golden Cock pub turn right, then fork left on to Butts Road, past St Lucius' Church, to return to the start.

JUDY WOODS

A stroll through some of the finest
beech woods in West Yorkshire.

Judy Woods are hemmed in by West Yorkshire villages but, nevertheless, are
some of the finest broadleaved woods in the county. To locals the whole area
is known as Judy Woods, recalling a woman called Judy North, or Gurt (Great)
Judy, who lived here during the 19th century.

Judy – A Local Legend
Her cottage was near to where Horse Close Bridge (usually known as Judy
Brig, or Bridge) spans Royds Hall Beck, the boundary between Calderdale
and Bradford. The North family occupied two cottages here and earned their
living weaving but in the 1830s opened their gardens to the public, and sold
spice sticks, ginger beer and Judy's renowned parkin to passers-by. Judy was
born Judith Stocks in 1795, and married into the family when she wedded
Joseph North in 1847. Joseph had several grown-up children, while Judy
had had five in a previous marriage; only one – John O'Judy – survived to
adulthood and he earned his keep selling vegetables. Judy died in 1870 and
her cottage was demolished the following year but she is immortalised in the
name of the woodlands and the bridge by which she lived.

The geology of Judy Woods is defined by layers of coal over a bedrock
of millstone grit. The coal has been mined for centuries; shallow depressions
visible on the woodland floor are the remains of bell pits, an early and
primitive method of mining. Coal and ironstone were extracted in the
18th century by the Low Moor Company, based just to the east of the
woods. The ironstone was used in forges at Low Moor – fired by the coal
dug here – to make cannons used at the Battle of Waterloo, during the
Napoleonic Wars.

A less obvious sign of local industry is the predominance of beech trees,
probably planted during the reign of Queen Victoria. These are a colourful
sight in autumn, when the leaves are turning from green to golden oranges,
reds and yellows, but were actually planted for a more prosaic purpose: to
provide the raw materials for the manufacture of spindles and bobbins for
the textile trade.

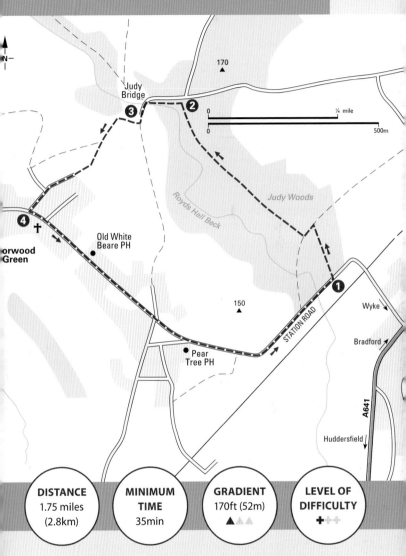

DISTANCE	MINIMUM TIME	GRADIENT	LEVEL OF DIFFICULTY
1.75 miles (2.8km)	35min	170ft (52m) ▲△△	✚✚✚

PATHS Woodland paths, good tracks and quiet roads; no stiles
LANDSCAPE Beech woodland and a quiet West Yorkshire village
SUGGESTED MAP OS Explorer 288 Bradford & Huddersfield
START/FINISH Grid reference: SE 147268
DOG FRIENDLINESS Dogs are free to exercise in the woods
PARKING On-street parking in Station Road, Norwood Green
PUBLIC TOILETS None on route

Opposite: Royds Hall Great Wood, part of Judy Woods

WALK 19 DIRECTIONS

❶ Walk through the kissing gate and follow a path signed to Woodside. After 220yds (201m) a path climbs off to the right but you should stay with the main, broad path, smooth enough to cater for wheelchair users, along its 940yd (860m) length. Of all the paths that score the woodland floor this is by far the finest and most scenic, passing beneath magnificent, towering specimens of beech, some of which are more than 200 years old.

❷ Where the engineered path terminates at a fence in the woodland

🔆 IN THE AREA
Bolling Hall Museum in Bradford provides a stark contrast with Judy North's simple life in the woods. Its period bedrooms give a glimpse of the life lived by wealthy Bradfordians through the 16th, 17th and 18th centuries.

🍴 EATING AND DRINKING
The Old White Beare began life in 1533 as a farm and ale house on the old packhorse route between Halifax and Leeds. After a fire in 1593, it was rebuilt using timbers from the Elizabethan galleon *Old White Beare*, one of the battleships which had led the defeat of the Spanish Armada five years earlier. Named in the ship's honour, the pub welcomes families with an á la carte restaurant menu, an alternative children's menu, four cask ales and space for dogs in the bar and traditional snug.

corner, turn left, down an enclosed path that parallels a rough track on your right, signed for Norwood Green. Within 550yds (503m) this descends to Judy Bridge, or Horse Close Bridge as it is also called.

❸ Ascend the lane beyond the bridge, ignoring an early fork, for 550yds (503m), after which it passes a series of garages to end at a junction with a road.

❹ Turn left, into the village of Norwood Green, passing the former Church of St George on your right and the Old White Beare pub on your left. Follow the road all the way through the village, past the Pear Tree pub and a warehouse on the right before rising gently back to the start point.

⚓ ON THE WALK
In the spring the beech woods are carpeted with bluebells. For most of the year these riotous flowers survive as tiny white bulbs about 6 inches (15cm) below the woodland floor. From late April until early June, the succulent green stems rise up to as much as 18 inches (45cm) in height. The individual flowers are very similar to the flowers of the garden hyacinth, though the bluebell's scent is a little more subtle.

THE VILLAGE THAT TITUS BUILT

The visionary benefactor who valued his workforce and won their respect in return.

Titus Salt was one of a handful of textile barons who sought to better the lives of their workforces. In the mid-19th century the majority of Bradford's textile workers endured appalling conditions. The boom in the industry had seen a migration of people into a city that lacked the infrastructure to support them. In 1849, during Salt's first term as city mayor, a cholera outbreak killed 420 people. Years before, in 1826, Salt had witnessed a Luddite-style riot at Horsfall's Mill in Bradford, during which troops opened fire on rioters, killing two youths.

An Ideal Village on the Banks of the Aire

Salt realised the benefits of a happy, healthy workforce. He began by taking his workers – up to 2,000 of them – on day trips into the Yorkshire Dales. But he had a greater vision in which his mills would be consolidated into one, at the heart of a new community.

He chose his green field site for its proximity to the waters of the Aire, needed for production, and the Leeds and Liverpool Canal, for distribution. Construction began in 1851 and when it opened on 20 September 1853 – Salt's 50th birthday – most of the 3,500 guests were employees.

Salt next set his architects to designing an entire village for his workforce. Albert Terrace was first to go up and the building of good quality housing continued for another 15 years. Salt provided shops, a church, schools, a club and institute for social and educational use, an infirmary… everything a town might need, other than pubs, which he saw as a source of social evil.

On his death at his mansion at Crow Nest in Lightcliffe, near Halifax, on 29 December 1876, his body was borne by procession to the family mausoleum at Saltaire Congregational Church. An estimated 100,000 people lined the route.

Today the village is a UNESCO World Heritage Site and the regenerated mill is home to shops, an art gallery devoted to the work of Bradford artist David Hockney, and many more attractions. Saltaire Mill, renamed Salt's Mill, is a remarkable memorial to a remarkable social pioneer.

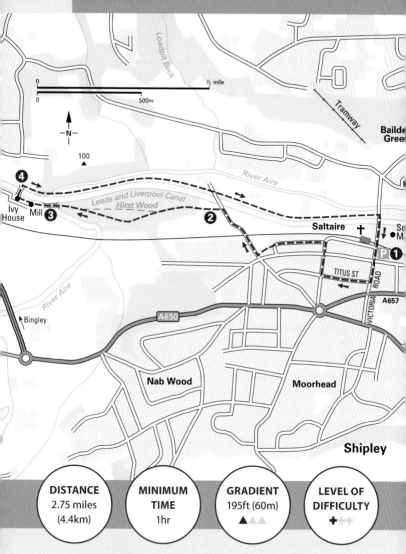

DISTANCE
2.75 miles
(4.4km)

MINIMUM TIME
1hr

GRADIENT
195ft (60m)
▲▲▲

LEVEL OF DIFFICULTY
✚✚✚

PATHS Roads, woodland paths and canal tow path; no stiles

LANDSCAPE Urban streets, woodland and waterways

SUGGESTED MAP OS Explorer 288 Bradford & Huddersfield

START/FINISH Grid reference: SE 139379

DOG FRIENDLINESS Dogs can exercise in the woods and on the canal tow path

PARKING Pay-and-display car park at corner of Victoria Road and Caroline Street, Saltaire; on-street parking near by **PUBLIC TOILETS** At car park at start

WALK 20 DIRECTIONS

1 Head up Victoria Road and turn right along Titus Street. Turn right at the end, down Albert Road, turning left near the bottom along Albert Avenue. At the far end take the footpath across the recreation ground, then turn right down Hirst Lane, crossing a railway bridge. After passing Hughes' bakery, head through the Hirst Wood car park.

2 Pass through a metal kissing gate into woodland. Keep left when the surfaced track forks after 100yds (91m), ignoring lesser paths which stray off to either side. When the trail branches in three directions, stay with the central option. Various tracks eventually converge and gently descend to a junction, where you turn right, following a Woodland Walk sign, to the canal tow path.

3 Turn left, over an aqueduct, after which the path drops to the left, then right, to run between walls past a converted canal warehouse and cottages, where it becomes a roughly surfaced track. After rounding appropriately named Ivy House, bear right to cross a canal bridge.

☙ ON THE WALK

Titus Salt and his wife Caroline had 11 children, and each has a street named after them in the village that Titus built. This walk visits the streets named after Titus and Caroline but those named for their offspring, and members of the Royal family, await your exploration. Also remembered are architects William Mawson and Henry Francis Lockwood.

4 Bear right along the tow path, canal on one side and the River Aire on the other, for 1.4 miles (2.25km), until you reach Saltaire, where Titus Salt's Congregational Church, his final resting place, stands on the opposite side of the canal. Leave the tow path by an Airedale Greenway information board and cross the bridge over the canal, continuing up Victoria Road back to the start of the walk.

☙ IN THE AREA

Victoria Hall, on Victoria Road, was originally Saltaire's Victoria Hall and Institute, a centre for culture and learning provided by Titus Salt for his villagers. It housed libraries, games rooms and even a dance hall.

🍴 EATING AND DRINKING

There's hardly a more appropriate place to refresh yourself after the walk than within Salt's Mill. On the second floor you'll find the contemporary Salt's Diner, which serves high quality hot meals and light refreshments. Children's portions are available. Titus probably wouldn't approve but the diner also serves wines and bottled beers. Open daily from 10am until 5.30pm (last food orders 4.30pm).

A floating ice-cream shop/café on the canal in Saltaire

ILKLEY MOOR AND THE TWELVE APOSTLES

Fantastic views and a stone circle on a wild moor
– don't forget your 'at!

Ilkley Moor is a long ridge of millstone grit, immediately to the south of Ilkley. With or without a hat, Ilkley Moor is a special place…not just for walkers, but for lovers of archaeological relics, too. These extensive heather moors are identified on maps as Rombald's Moor, after a legendary giant who once roamed the area. But, thanks to the famous song – Yorkshire's unofficial anthem – Ilkley Moor is how it will always be known.

Ancient Occupation and Curative Waters

The Twelve Apostles is a ring of Bronze Age standing stones sited close to the meeting of two ancient routes across the moor. If you expect to find something of Stonehenge proportions, you will be disappointed. The 12 slabs of millstone grit (there were more originally, probably 20, with one at the centre) are arranged in a circle approximately 50ft (15m) in diameter. The tallest is little more than 3ft (1m). The circle is, nevertheless, a genuinely ancient monument.

There are milestones too, dating from more recent times, which would have given comfort and guidance to travellers across these lonely moors. In addition to the Pancake Stone, seen on this walk, there are dozens of other natural gritstone rock formations. The biggest and best known are the Cow and Calf, close to the start of this walk, where climbers practise their holds and rope work. The Cow and Calf used to be a complete family unit but the rock known as the Bull was broken up to provide building stone.

A guidebook of 1829 described Ilkley as a little village. It was the discovery of mineral springs that transformed it into a prosperous spa town. Dr William Mcleod arrived here in 1847, recognised the town's potential and spent the next 25 years creating a place where well-heeled hypochondriacs could 'take the waters' in upmarket surroundings.

Dr Mcleod recognised the curative properties of cold water. He vigorously promoted what he called the 'Ilkley Cure', a strict regime of exercise and cold baths. Luxurious hotels known as 'hydros', precursors of today's health farms, sprang up around the town to cater for the influx of visitors.

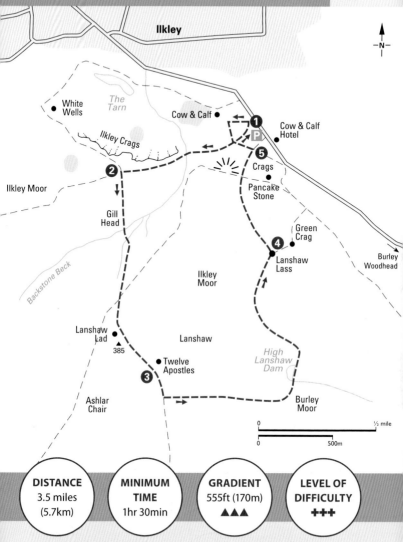

Ilkley

White Wells

The Tarn

Cow & Calf

Cow & Calf Hotel

P ①

⑤

Crags

Ilkley Crags

Pancake Stone

②

Ilkley Moor

Gill Head

Green Crag

④

Lanshaw Lass

Burley Woodhead

Backstone Beck

Ilkley Moor

Lanshaw Lad

385

Lanshaw

Twelve Apostles

③

High Lanshaw Dam

Ashlar Chair

Burley Moor

0   ½ mile
0   500m

—N—

DISTANCE
3.5 miles
(5.7km)

MINIMUM TIME
1hr 30min

GRADIENT
555ft (170m)
▲▲▲

LEVEL OF DIFFICULTY
+++

PATHS Obvious moorland paths, great potential for mud; no stiles
LANDSCAPE Open heather moorland and gritstone crags
SUGGESTED MAP OS Explorer 297, Lower Wharfedale & Washburn Valley
START/FINISH Grid reference: SE 132467 **DOG FRIENDLINESS** Plenty of
opportunity for exercise but dogs should be under close control where sheep
graze **PARKING** Cow and Calf rocks car park, off Hangingstone Road, Ilkley
PUBLIC TOILETS Ilkley town centre, on main car park **NOTE** As the wildest walk in
the book, this route is best tackled in fine weather

WALK 21 DIRECTIONS

❶ Follow the path from the car park towards the Cow and Calf rocks, bearing left up an intersecting flag path just before the rocks. At the crossroads turn right and continue ahead on a peaty path through heather. Ignoring any side trails or lesser forks, the path dips to cross Backstone Beck. Maintain your direction on the opposite bank, ignoring a maze of side-trails, and aim for the outcrops you can see along the moorland edge ahead. Follow the wide moorland track to a crossroads marked by the first, and lower, of two cairns.

❷ Turn left here, on a similarly good path across the wild heart of the moor, pausing only to cross the beck at Gill Head. Where the path forks, keep ahead, intermittently on deteriorating boardwalk. The path crests close to the boundary stone known as Lanshaw Lad – you'll meet his sister in a short while. Just ahead, to the left of the path, is the Twelve Apostles.

❸ Continue past the circle for 130yds (119m), to a cairn. Turn left here, on a jeep track which follows a moorland drain, indicated by a broken line of rushes. After 875yds (800m) bear left, down a muddy slope, to the wall of High Lanshaw Dam – take care as the dam's outflow can be deep in places after prolonged rain. Walk along the dam wall as it sweeps round to the left and pick up the marshy trail beyond, which bears right as it meets another track coming from the dam. Aim for a prominent marker post on the skyline not far ahead. Close to this post lies the toppled boundary stone Lanshaw Lass.

❹ The path beyond, now indicated by occasional wooden posts, offers more spectacular views of Wharfedale. The path forks as it spills over the edge, by the boulders of Green Crag. Bear left, away from the post-marked path for one more heavily used. After 550yds (503m) bear right at a junction to descend a groove towards The Cow and Calf Hotel, seen beyond – the prominent balanced rock on the moor edge away to your right is known as the Pancake Stone, and bears several cup and ring markings.

❺ Before reaching the road near the hotel, a bold track cuts across your path. Bear left along this, and keep ahead at the next crossroads, to turn right at the junction of several tracks just beyond, to return to the car park.

> ⑪ **EATING AND DRINKING**
> The refreshment kiosk on the car park at the start is very well stocked with confectionary, light snacks, drinks and a surprising range of speciality coffees. It's also a good source of walking guides and other information. The nearby Cow and Calf Hotel offers fresh seasonal food and a children's menu, as well as constantly changing cask ales.

Opposite: Cow and Calf Rocks

TRAMWAY AND BAILDON MOOR

A glimpse of moorland and a traditional rural playground for the mill workers of Shipley and Saltaire.

For the people of Shipley and Saltaire, Baildon Moor has traditionally represented a taste of the countryside on their doorsteps. Millhands could leave the mills and cramped terraced streets behind, and breathe clean Pennine air. They could listen to the song of the skylark and the bubbling cry of the curlew. There were heather moors to tramp across, gritstone rocks to scramble up and, at Shipley Glen, springy sheep-grazed turf on which to spread out a picnic blanket. There was also a funfair to visit – not a small affair either but a veritable theme park.

Toward the end of the 19th century Shipley Glen was owned by a Colonel Maude, who created a number of attractions, including the Switchback Railway, Marsden's Menagerie, the Horse Tramway and the Aerial Runway. More sedate pleasures were found at the Camera Obscura, the boating lake in the Japanese garden, and the Temperance Tea Room and Coffee House.

The Shipley Glen Tramway

Sam Wilson, a local entrepreneur, played his part in developing Shipley Glen. In 1895 he created the Shipley Glen Tramway. Saltaire people could now stroll through Roberts Park, past the steely-gazed statue of Sir Titus Salt, and enjoy the tramride to the top of the glen. Thousands of people would clamber, each weekend, on to the little cable-hauled 'toast-rack' cars. As one car went up the hill, another car would descend on an adjacent track.

In commercial terms, the heyday of Shipley Glen was during the Edwardian era. On busy days, as many as 17,000 people would take the tramway up to the pleasure gardens. Losing out to more sophisticated entertainments, however, Shipley Glen went into a slow decline. Sadly, all the attractions are now gone, but you can still take the ride on the tramway – it runs every weekend and bank holiday afternoons throughout the year. There is an attractive souvenir shop at the top, while the bottom station houses a small museum and replica Edwardian shop.

The Old Glen House is still a popular pub, though the former Temperance Tea Room and Coffee House is now the Bracken Hall Countryside Centre.

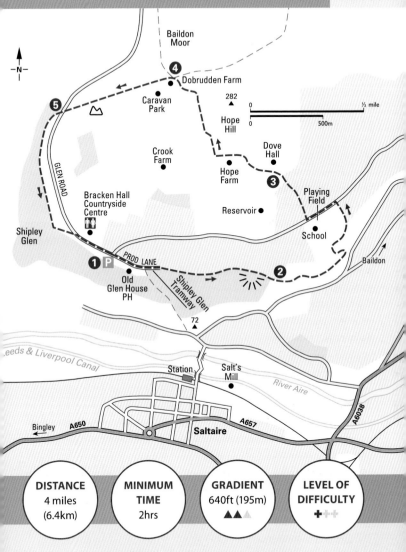

Baildon Moor

4 Dobrudden Farm

Caravan Park

5

282 ▲

Hope Hill

Dove Hall

Crook Farm

Hope Farm

3

Playing Field

GLEN ROAD

Bracken Hall Countryside Centre

Reservoir

School

Shipley Glen

1 P

PROD LANE

2

Baildon

Old Glen House PH

Shipley Glen Tramway

72 ▲

Leeds & Liverpool Canal

Station

Salt's Mill

River Aire

A6038

Bingley

A650

A657

Saltaire

0 ½ mile
0 500m

–N–

DISTANCE
4 miles
(6.4km)

MINIMUM TIME
2hrs

GRADIENT
640ft (195m)
▲▲

LEVEL OF DIFFICULTY
✚✚

PATHS Moor and field paths, no stiles

LANDSCAPE Moorland, fields and gritstone rocks

SUGGESTED MAP OS Explorer 288 Bradford & Huddersfield

START/FINISH Grid reference: SE 131389

DOG FRIENDLINESS Can be off lead except in Saltaire

PARKING On Glen Road, between Bracken Hall Countryside Centre and Old Glen House pub **PUBLIC TOILETS** At Bracken Hall Countryside Centre; also in Saltaire

WALK 22 DIRECTIONS

❶ Walk down Glen Road, passing the Old Glen House pub. Continue as the road becomes Prod Lane, signed as a cul-de-sac. Where the road ends at the entrance to the Shipley Glen Tramway, keep straight ahead to locate an enclosed path to the right of a house. Follow this path, with houses on your left, and woodland to your right. As you come to a metal barrier, ignore a path to the left. Keep straight on downhill. In 100yds (91m) beyond the barrier, there is a choice of paths; bear left here, contouring the steep hillside and soon getting good views over Saltaire, Shipley and the Aire Valley.

❷ At a fork above a building, take the right branch, which undulates beneath a quarried sandstone cliff. When you later come to an area of open heath, with panoramic views, take a set of stone steps, with metal handrails, up to the top of the cliff. Turn right on a path between chain-link fences, which takes you around school playing fields, to meet a road. Walk left along the road for 150yds (137m). When you are level with the school on your left, cross the road and take a narrow, enclosed path on the right, between houses. Walk gradually uphill, crossing a road in a housing estate and picking up the enclosed path again. Soon, at a kissing gate, you emerge into pasture.

❸ Go half left, uphill, to a kissing gate at the top-left corner of the field. Head out to join an access track along the field top to Hope Farm. Walk past the buildings on a cinder track, leaving just before its end on to a bridleway through a gate on the right. Beyond the next gate you come out on to Baildon Moor. Your path is clear, following a wall to your left. Keep straight on, as the wall curves to the left, towards the next farm (and caravan park). Cross a metalled farm track and curve left to follow the boundary wall of Dobrudden Farm.

❹ Walk gradually downhill towards Bingley in the valley. When the wall bears left, keep straight ahead, through bracken, more steeply downhill. Cross a metalled track and carry on down to meet Glen Road again.

❺ Follow the path along the rocky edge of wooded Shipley Glen, leading you back to the Bracken Hall Countryside Centre and your car.

🍴 EATING AND DRINKING

Sir Titus Salt wouldn't allow public houses in Saltaire, but that prohibition didn't extend to Shipley Glen, where the Old Glen House, near the upper tramway station is open daily for lunch and evening meals on all but Sunday. Choose from an array of sandwiches or the home-cooked specials, where fish dishes are popular. It also boasts an authentic cappuccino machine and features guest beers from around the county.

ANCIENT HALLS OF COLEY

Tales of uncivil bombardments, champion archers
and ghosts abound on this pastoral stroll.

Coley is a peaceful backwater on a hill high to the north-east of Halifax, its church tower visible for miles around from many directions. It is surrounded by pastures and secretive wooded valleys which conceal exquisite waterfalls.

Ancient halls dot the area and this gentle walk visits two of them. Both are rumoured to have had secret tunnels between them and the chapel that once stood close to the site of the present Church of St John the Baptist.

Two Ancient Halls

Coley Hall has had a colourful history. Records for the site go back as far as 1277 when a medieval priory is thought to have occupied this location. Parts of the present building date back to 1572, though the bulk was built around 1640. Not long after, during the English Civil Wars, it was bombarded by passing Parliamentarian troops after its owner, Captain Langdale Sunderland, sided with the Royalists. The south frontage had to be rebuilt.

From 1662 to 1665, the hall was home to leading Nonconformist minister Oliver Heywood. Heywood was unconventional, rejecting state interference in religious affairs and was excommunicated in 1662. When the Five Mile Act of 1665 forbade excommunicated ministers from preaching within five miles (8km) of their former parish, Heywood seized the opportunity to spread the Nonconformist cause, travelling thousands of miles as an itinerant evangelist and founded a new chapel in nearby Northowram.

Coley Hall was semi-derelict by the 1960s when it was bought by Richard Pickles, who set about restoring it. In doing so he seems to have awoken spirits from Heywood's time. Royalist Cavaliers have been encountered in more than one room, while a white lady is said to haunt the main staircase.

Wynteredge Hall is so-called because it sits on the edge of a hill and bears the brunt of chilling winter gusts. Parts of the building are believed to date back as far as 1371 though the main body was rebuilt in the 1640s. John King, of Hipperholme, who lived in the hall until 1675 was regarded as the best English archer of his day. As well as entertaining King Charles I with his skills, he is said to have won many wagers during the civil wars.

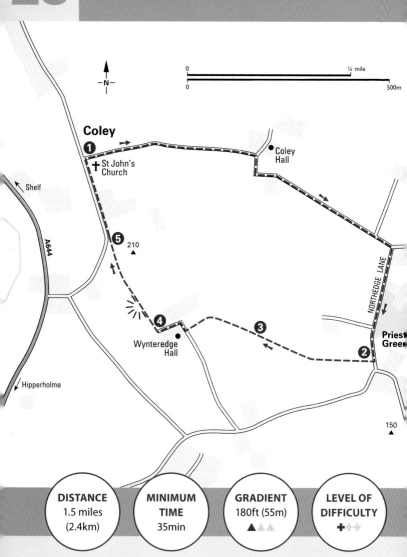

DISTANCE
1.5 miles
(2.4km)

MINIMUM TIME
35min

GRADIENT
180ft (55m)
▲▲▲

LEVEL OF DIFFICULTY
✚✚✚

PATHS Good tracks, quiet country lanes and field paths; 4 stiles
LANDSCAPE Pastoral countryside **SUGGESTED MAP** OS Explorer 288 Bradford
& Huddersfield **START/FINISH** Grid reference: SE 124269
DOG FRIENDLINESS Dogs should be under control throughout and on lead
on farmland **PARKING** On-street parking outside St John's Church, Coley. Park
considerately, especially when services are being held
PUBLIC TOILETS None on route

WALK 23 DIRECTIONS

❶ Take the lane to the left of the church. After 440yds (402m) this kinks right, around Coley Hall, then continues to a T-junction. Cross over and turn right, along Northedge Lane, for 300yds (274m).

❷ Immediately before the junction with Syke Lane, re-cross and take a stile through a hedge, where a waymarker indicates that the field path ahead is part of the Brighouse Boundary Walk. Ascend the field ahead, passing beneath power lines, and cross a wooden stile through a wall ahead. Bear diagonally right across the subsequent field, aiming to meet the power line again in the top right corner.

❸ Pass between old stone gate posts and continue in the same direction, following the power line. In the top field corner climb a wooden step stile by a metal gate and turn right, along a surfaced driveway, then left beyond the outbuildings of Wynteredge Hall into a walled lane at the back of a large stone barn.

🦴 ON THE WALK

The ornate, 17th-century gateway at Coley Hall might have survived an attack during the English Civil War but the elements have since eroded its fine detail somewhat. The date stone at the top of the arch reads 1649 and as well as the double-headed cross motif of the Order of St John, the arch bears representations of dogs and other animals.

❹ Pass through a kissing gate at the end of the lane and turn right, along the brow of Wynteredge Hill. This ridge offers great views across what is known locally as Chelsea Valley, to the villages of Northowram and Southowram. On clear days, Crow Hill in the Calder Valley, and Manshead Hill above Cragg Vale are visible, and you might even glimpse Almondbury Hill and Victoria Tower above Huddersfield, as well as the high moors of the Peak District even further away.

❺ The ridge path ends at a stone step stile beyond which you should continue ahead for 160yds (146m), back to the church.

🍴 EATING AND DRINKING

Across the road from the church in Coley, a narrow snicket down the side of the graveyard takes you to The Brown Horse inn, an English pub with a taste for the exotic: in addition to the traditional meals served seven days a week, specials regularly include the unexpected, such as kangaroo, wild boar and Caribbean butter fish. There's also a full children's menu. Dogs are only allowed inside when food's not being served but there's an enclosed beer garden. A selection of Yorkshire cask ales is also offered.

CALDER & HEBBLE AND THE CALDERDALE WAY

A peaceful nature reserve offers tranquillity between industrious Brighouse and Elland.

Never head of Cromwell Bottom? Well, the birds have. In fact more than 200 species have been recorded at this secretive reserve, sandwiched between the River Calder and the Calder and Hebble Navigation, just outside Brighouse.

A mix of woodland, wetland and grassland, Cromwell Bottom is regarded as one of Calderdale's most important sites for nature conservation, boasting an extraordinary diversity of flora and fauna. Around 130 species of plant have been recorded, along with amphibians, including frogs, toads and newts, mammals such as roe deer, and insects including dragonflies and damselflies. Butterflies recorded here include orange tip, peacock, brimstone and small tortoiseshell, while the list of birds seems almost endless though its thoroughness is no doubt helped by the fact that the Royal Society for the Protection of Birds once had its north-west office in the nearby mill complex.

Along the River Calder

The Calder and Hebble Navigation was one of the last canals in England to carry freight. It developed during the 18th century, when waterways became important for the distribution of raw materials and finished goods.

In this case, it began not as a canal but as an attempt to improve the River Calder for boats by bypassing non-navigable stretches with man-made diversions between Brighouse, Elland and Sowerby Bridge. Despite strong opposition from mill owners, who feared the works might reduce the power available from the river for their mills, Parliament granted permission for the river to be improved in 1758. Work began in 1761, under the command of canal engineers John Smeaton and James Brindley. The 24-mile (39km) length of the Calder and Hebble Navigation between Wakefield and Sowerby Bridge opened in 1770 and over successive years further lengths of river were bypassed, until the majority of the route was man-made, including the straight-as-a-dye stretch between Brighouse and Elland followed by this walk.

While other canals were put out of business by the development of the railways, the Calder and Hebble continued to bear commercial freight until the 1980s, when road haulage finally beat it into submission.

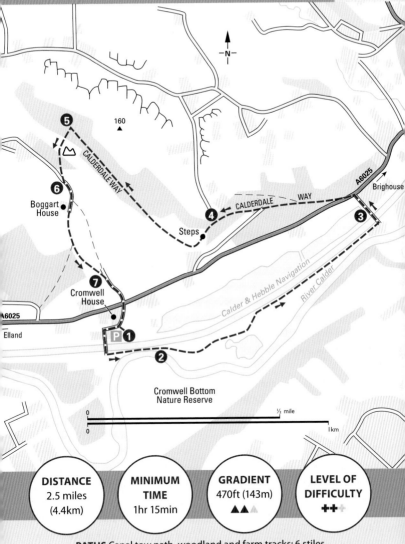

160 ▲

CALDERDALE WAY

5

6
Boggart
House

CALDERDALE WAY

4

Steps

A6025
Brighouse

3

Calder & Hebble Navigation

River Calder

7
Cromwell
House

A6025
Elland

P 1

2

Cromwell Bottom
Nature Reserve

0   ½ mile
0   1 km

DISTANCE	**MINIMUM TIME**	**GRADIENT**	**LEVEL OF DIFFICULTY**
2.5 miles (4.4km)	1hr 15min	470ft (143m) ▲▲△	✚✚✚

PATHS Canal tow path, woodland and farm tracks; 6 stiles

LANDSCAPE Peaceful canal side, wooded valley sides

SUGGESTED MAP OS Explorer 288 Bradford & Huddersfield

START/FINISH Grid reference: SE 124223

DOG FRIENDLINESS Dogs should be under control in the nature reserve but
are free to exercise in the woodlands across the valley **PARKING** Small car park
behind Cromwell House, off the A6025 Elland Road, Brighouse

PUBLIC TOILETS None on route

Walk
24
Cromwell Bottom

WALK 24 DIRECTIONS

❶ Take the trail from the far end of the car park, immediately turning left on to a footbridge across the Calder and Hebble Navigation. Descend steps and turn right onto the tow path.

❷ About 65yds (60m) after passing between a pair of gate posts either side of the tow path, turn right through a kissing gate, on to a path that winds through Cromwell Bottom Nature Reserve. Bear left at the first junction, soon passing a large area of reeds on your right, before rejoining the tow path, via another kissing gate, at Cromwell Lock. Bear right again, past Cromwell Bridge, to the next set of lock gates, Brookfoot Locks. Cross a stone bridge and bear right to a road.

❸ Turn left here, along the edge of an industrial estate, to the main A6025 road. Cross carefully and take the stile opposite into a lane climbing away from the road; though unsigned, this is the Calderdale Way. Where the track forks 220yds (201m) later, keep left. Ignore the next left turn and stay with the track, marked with the 'CW' brand on a wall corner. The walled lane gently rises to pass beneath power lines.

❹ Where the track turns off right, climb a step stile by a gate in the bend ahead, and descend a long flight of steps toward a farmyard. At the foot of the steps, turn right up a walled lane into oak woodland. Stay on the main woodland path, ignoring any side trails.

❺ When you're 710yds (649m) into the woodland, where a track comes down the slope from your right to cross yours, look for the faint path down the slope to your left. Descend this to a wooden stile, beyond which the path fords a stream. Climb the grassy bank opposite, which is steep and can be slippery after rain, trending left into trees and rising to pass through a stone stile into a walled lane.

❻ Turn left, downhill, to Boggart House. Beyond, the route continues ahead as a narrower path, stepping over a wooden barrier to descend an old stone cart track through woods for 260yds (238m). A stile on your left then takes you off, on to a woodland path, part of the Brighouse Boundary Walk. It descends, alongside a deep, ravine-like clough, to a junction of tracks.

❼ Turn right here, down a lane, to the A6025 Brighouse–Elland road. Cross with care and head down the lane directly opposite back to the car park.

> ⓨ **EATING AND DRINKING**
> The Colliers Arms, which backs on to the Calder and Hebble at Elland, is named after the coal-hauling bargees who once moored their boats behind the pub. Today it welcomes hungry and thirsty walkers and their dogs, with meals served lunchtime and evening most days.

THE SWASTIKA STONE AND WHITE WELLS

An ancient symbol for luck or prehistoric graffiti?
Judge for yourself!

For millennia before the National Socialist Workers Party adopted it in 1920 and corrupted its reputation for all time, the swastika was a symbol of peace. Today we inevitably associate the symbol with the German Nazi party and the horrors of the Second World War. In Hindu culture it is a symbol that occurs in holy texts, standing for luck or rebirth. It occurs in Buddhism and the peaceful Indian Jainism religion, as well as other Asian and European cultures. So what is a 3,000 to 4,000-year-old swastika doing carved into a gritstone rock above the town of Ilkley? The answer is, of course, that no-one has a clue.

The Swastika Stone

The Swastika Stone is the best known of Ilkley Moor's hundreds of examples of prehistoric rock art, though it is thought to be slightly more recent than the majority of cup and ring markings carved into rocks all over the moor. It depicts a shape with four curved arms, each 'holding' a cup mark, with another cup mark in each 'armpit', and one in the centre. The cups line up in two rows of five, meeting in the centre like a cross.

The artist who carved it had probably never seen the swastika-style Camunian rose, carved into a rocks in Sellero, Italy, or the other rose designs in Val Camonica, but their work is virtually identical. The rose has been traditionally held to be a 'good luck' symbol but has also been interpreted as an image of the sun radiating life. Similar carvings are found elsewhere in Europe, including Sweden and Portugal, and one has even been reported in Australia, near Brisbane. Perhaps Ilkley's Swastika Stone is an international symbol of good luck, perhaps it illustrates the heavens revolving around the sun. Perhaps it's 3,000-year-old graffiti.

You're welcome to form your own opinion when you see the stone but note that the one close to the railings on Woodhouse Moor isn't the original but is a modern reproduction, provided to offer clarity to the design; the real Swastika Stone lies directly behind it and is slightly less distinguishable thanks to 3,000 years – or is it 4,000? – of exposure to the elements.

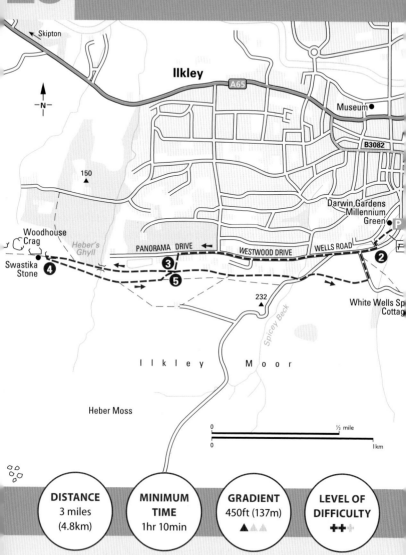

DISTANCE
3 miles (4.8km)

MINIMUM TIME
1hr 10min

GRADIENT
450ft (137m) ▲▲▲

LEVEL OF DIFFICULTY
+++

PATHS Quiet lanes, peaty paths and good moorland tracks; no stiles
LANDSCAPE Urban fringe and open moor
SUGGESTED MAP OS Explorer 297 Lower Wharfedale & the Washburn Valley
START/FINISH Grid reference: SE 117471 **DOG FRIENDLINESS** Dogs should be under close control where sheep graze on the moor **PARKING** Darwin Gardens Millennium Green car park, Wells Road, Ilkley **PUBLIC TOILETS** White Wells Spa Cottage (off main route) or Ilkley's main town centre car park

WALK 25 DIRECTIONS

1 Take the ascending path from the far-right corner of the car park, heading right at a fork, over a footbridge, then left at the subsequent three junctions to a driveway. Cross the grassy area in front of you to Wells Road.

2 Turn right along the pavement, keeping ahead into Westwood Drive when the road forks by Westwood Lodge. Maintain direction when the road bends off to the right, to enter quiet Westwood Drive, which in turn becomes Panorama Drive. Some 385yds (352m) later, by a house named Shamble Corner, take a walled path to a wooden gate.

3 Pass through this into open country, turning right, past a small reservoir. A footbridge carries the path over waterfalls at Heber's Ghyll. The less distinct path beyond soon passes through a latched metal gate and crosses a second stream. Bear left at a junction encountered after 30yds (27m) to follow a moor-edge track

---

EATING AND DRINKING

White Wells Spa Cottage is something of a walkers' institution on Ilkley Moor. When the flags is flying you'll find snacks and drinks available – that's usually weekends, bank holidays (except Christmas Day) and school holidays. When the flag isn't flying, you'll find a variety of pubs, restaurants, bistros and sandwich bars in Ilkley.

---

right, to a small fenced enclosure on Woodhouse Crag, within which lies the Swastika Stone.

4 Stepping away from the crag edge you'll find a broad track. Take this, heading back in the direction you came from, enjoying fine views of the Cow and Calf rocks far ahead and, to your left, Wharfedale. After passing through a gate and crossing a beck, the trail brings you to the gate encountered at the end of Point **2**.

ON THE WALK

The prehistoric artist who carved the Swastika Stone would have enjoyed a tremendous view from his perch on the edge of Woodhouse Crag. Gazing directly north across Wharfedale and the town of Ilkley, his eyes would have alighted on Barden Moor and Simon's Seat, Beamsley Beacon and Blubberhouses Moor, Stainburn Moor and Almscliffe Crag.

---

5 Don't go through the gate this time. Turn right and 700yds (640m) later fork left, below a small car park, to cross Spicey Beck and meet a road beyond. Cross and hop up the bank opposite to find the path's continuation. Turn left for 550yds (503m) to its intersection with the driveway for White Wells Spa Cottage. If you're in need of refreshment and a flag is flying, turn right. Otherwise, turn left, down to Wells Road, and bear right there to return to the car park.

THE LAKE DISTRICT IN MINIATURE

Explore the water gatherer's wooded landscape.

You don't have to drive all the way to Cumbria to enjoy a landscape of large water features. At the head of the Holme Valley, Kirklees has its own Lake District in miniature.

To the south of Holmbridge, four reservoirs occupy an area of less than 1.5 square miles (4sq km). They were built over a period of 54 years: Yateholme, which currently holds 91.3 million gallons (415 million litres), was the first in 1878, while Brownhill (266 million gallons/1,210 million litres), closest to the village, was completed in 1932. The other two, Riding Wood (52 million gallons/236 million litres) and Ramsden, (87 million gallons/396 million litres) were completed in 1883 and 1892 respectively.

A Watery Landscape

The dams lie across several streams, the names of some of which – Gusset Dike and Boggery Dike – give a clue to the nature of the ground. Fortunately most of the walk follows a good track and only on one section are you likely to encounter boggy terrain.

Those streams drain the highest ground in West Yorkshire: the moorland slopes that rise ahead of you as you pass Yateholme Reservoir are Holme Moss, the flanks of Black Hill, the notoriously boggy summit of which is 1,909ft (582m) above sea level. Its peat hags and mires were long-feared by Pennine Way walkers until the worst sections were improved by the laying of stone flags, imported from demolished cotton mills, across the peat.

The radio transmitter on Holme Moss stands 750ft-tall (228m). Coupled with its altitude of 1,719 feet (524m) above sea level, that makes it one of the highest in the country – so high that the television signal it used to transmit could be received on the Isle of Man, and in Dublin in Ireland. Today it broadcasts signals for a number of digital and analogue BBC radio stations, its TV duties having been adopted by Emley Moor transmitter.

The reservoirs' waters flow out towards Holmbridge, where they join with those of Marsden Clough to become the River Holme, which flows through the valley to meet the Colne near Huddersfield town centre.

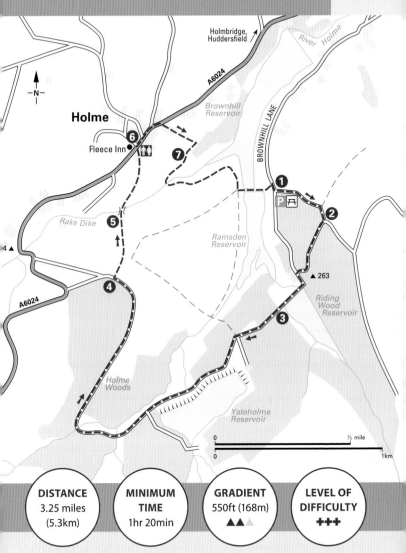

DISTANCE
3.25 miles
(5.3km)

MINIMUM TIME
1hr 20min

GRADIENT
550ft (168m)
▲▲▲

LEVEL OF DIFFICULTY
+++

PATHS Mostly good reservoir tracks with one short muddy section; 6 stiles
LANDSCAPE Wooded valley sides, open pasture and reservoirs
SUGGESTED MAP OS Explorer 288 Bradford & Huddersfield, or OL1 The Peak
District (Dark Peak area) **START/FINISH** Grid reference: SE 115056
DOG FRIENDLINESS Dogs can be off-lead much of the way but should be on
lead through livestock **PARKING** Car park at end of Brownhill Lane, south of
Holmbridge **PUBLIC TOILETS** In Holme village, opposite the Fleece Inn

WALK 26 DIRECTIONS

❶ Walk through the picnic area next to the car park and cross the stile into a lane. After climbing for 80yds (73m), pass between stone gate posts and swing right, on a grassy track and over a stream, past a conifer plantation. Continue uphill on a wide track, which re-crosses the stream, to a junction. Waymarked trails continue ahead and left here; your way, however, turns right, between posts. After 90yds (82m) you come to a junction with a well-defined rough track.

❷ Turn right, downhill, into the conifers, occasionally glimpsing Ramsden Reservoir through the trees. After 300yds (274m) the track reaches a junction, by an isolated house. Turn left to cross the dam wall of Riding Wood Reservoir, high above Ramsden Reservoir on your right, with views across to the village of Holme.

❸ Continue along the track beyond the dam, past the huge retaining walls of Yateholme Reservoir. Although this track is very quiet and rarely used, be aware that timber-hauling lorries and machinery might occasionally come this way. After crossing several streams the track crosses to the opposite side of the clough, gently climbing to offer fine views down the Holme Valley.

❹ About a 1.3 miles (2.1km) after crossing Riding Wood Reservoir, a public footpath sign directs you off the track right, down a boggy field, paralleling the wall 20yds (18m) to the right: scout around for the driest ground. Cross a dilapidated wall after 140yds (128m) and turn left along it to cross a wooden stile, into oak and birch woodland and down stone steps.

❺ Cross Rake Dike on a wooden footbridge. An obvious path slants right, up the opposite bank, climbs three fields and passes through a gate into a garden, and out the other side. Ascend a driveway to emerge on a road opposite Holme's Fleece Inn.

❻ Turn right, past the public toilets and phone box. Just 65yds (60m) past Holme Sunday School turn right on a public footpath, past Underhill to your right. Beyond a narrow metal gate, the path drops along the left edge of a field, passing through a wooden gate half-way down to continue within an enclosed path. Beyond a stile, turn right through a narrow gap in the wall to drop diagonally down the next field.

❼ The path, beyond a stile at the bottom, follows the wall on the right, above woodland, before descending to cross Rake Dike above a small waterfall. Beyond, it ascends a rough stone path back to the treeline, with occasional views of Brownhill Reservoir, then drops again out of the woodland. Cross the face of Ramsden Reservoir's dam wall and bear left at the end up to the road, then right, back to the car park.

Opposite: Rake Dike in autumn

CHELLOW DENE

A gentle walk around one
of Bradford's favourite reservoirs.

Chellow Dene is a fine spot for a walk at any time of year. In autumn however, when the leaves on the beech trees that surround the valley's two reservoirs are turning to bronze and gold, the area looks magnificent.

The Victorian reservoirs were built by the Bradford Corporation to ensure a supply of water for the city's burgeoning population. At the time people were flooding to the city, looking for work in the flourishing textile industry but the overcrowding was having serious effects on people's health, and clean drinking water and sanitation were vital if disease was to be avoided.

A Wildlife Corridor

First to be built was the upper reservoir, in 1844; the lower dam followed in 1853. Apart from water, being so close to the centre of Bradford, the reservoirs provide a green lung just a short distance from the city's hustle and bustle. The valley also acts as a wildlife corridor, along which birds and mammals can move freely within the surrounding built-up areas.

The open water attracts birds such as the heron and great crested grebe, while kingfishers have been seen on Chellow Dene Beck, the stream that feeds the dams. The surrounding woodlands are home to nuthatch, green and great spotted woodpecker as well as goldcrest. Even more exciting visitors have included buzzard and osprey.

A conservation group, The Friends of Chellow Dene, was formed in 2009 to help maintain this rural oasis. The group works with rangers to encourage wildlife by providing bat and bird boxes, creating nature trails and more.

Chellow Dene Beck joins other streams beyond the dams to form Bradford Beck, on which the city of Bradford – 'Broad-ford' – was founded. Its fate emphasises the value of open spaces such as Chellow Dene. For a while Bradford's industry depended on the beck but the need for waterpower diminished with the advent of electricity. As the beck became less vital, and heavily polluted, it was channelled underground and forgotten. For almost its entire length, to its confluence with the River Aire at Shipley, the beck now rarely sees the light of day.

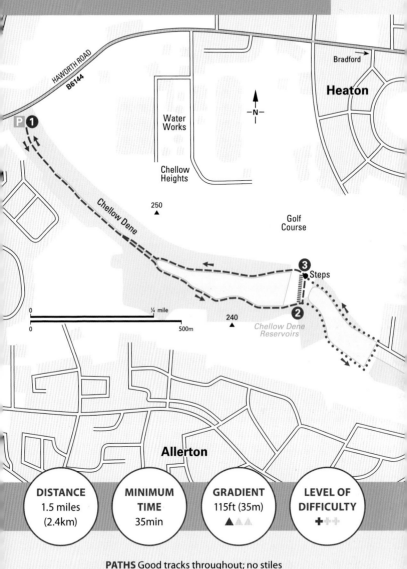

DISTANCE
1.5 miles
(2.4km)

MINIMUM TIME
35min

GRADIENT
115ft (35m)
▲▲▲

LEVEL OF DIFFICULTY
✚✚✚

PATHS Good tracks throughout; no stiles
LANDSCAPE Reservoirs set in beech and oak woodland
SUGGESTED MAP OS Explorer 288 Bradford & Huddersfield
START/FINISH Grid reference: SE 111352
DOG FRIENDLINESS Dogs are free to exercise in the woodlands
PARKING Car park off the B6144 Haworth Road, near its junction with the B6146
PUBLIC TOILETS None on route

WALK 27 DIRECTIONS

❶ Leave the car park on the track from the information board. Head into woodland and keep ahead at the junction encountered after 66yds (60m). When the path forks either side of a brook, take the right-hand option; don't be tempted to cross the stepping stones near the head of the dam. The path follows the south side of the reservoir to the dam wall. There are plenty of birds and other wildlife to look out for here, so it is worth having binoculars and a field guide with you.

❷ Here you can choose to either cross the dam wall and complete the walk up the opposite side, or lengthen the walk by circumnavigating the lower dam, regaining the upper reservoir path afterwards via a flight of steps up the dam wall; this will add 0.5 miles (800m) distance and around 10 minutes to your walk, and a mere 40ft (15m) ascent.

❸ At the far end of the upper dam wall, simply follow the north shore, regaining the outward path just beyond the top end of the dam to return to the car park.

🍴 EATING AND DRINKING

The Prune Park pub, in nearby Prune Park Lane, Wilsden, welcomes walkers and families, whether they want a fine pub meal, a drink or simply a cup of tea and a rest after their exertions. Meals are served every day of the week and there's a specific kids' menu.

⊘ IN THE AREA

Cartwright Hall, about a mile (1.6km) from the city centre, is Bradford's art gallery and, as befits a place with such a diverse cultural heritage, its collection includes works by artists of many cultures, from around the world. The museum is set in one of Bradford's largest parks, which also features a boating lake, water gardens, tennis courts and play areas. The park, which is worthy of a good exploratory walk in its own right, is open 24 hours a day, year-round.

🦌 ON THE WALK

Chellow Dene's woodlands are ideal habitat for roe deer, the smaller of Britain's two true native deer species. These shy, solitary creatures come together in small groups in winter, when locals enjoy watching them graze at the woodland edge. Under the trees, however, they're hard to spot as their ruddy brown coats blend perfectly with the leaf litter; you might just spot their white rumps as they bound away.

THE 1852 BILBERRY DAM DISASTER

How poor workmanship damned
the lives of dozens.

It's a peaceful spot today, cherished by passing Kirklees Way walkers and those who enjoy the encircling paths created by Yorkshire Water. Digley Reservoir, which drains an area of some 14,000 acres (5,670ha) of moorland, is a relative newcomer as Pennine dams go, having been built in 1952.

The reservoir it was built to supersede, however, earned a dark place in the history books, a century earlier. Bilberry Dam, which lies upstream of Digley Reservoir, burst its embankment on 5 February 1852, causing one of the worst ever losses of life from a flood.

Plans for the dam were prepared in 1838 by engineer George Leather. Against his advice, the commissioners employed Messrs Sharp and Sons, of Dewsbury, who had submitted the lowest tender (£9,324) to construct the dam. Leather wasn't present when the 300ft-wide (91m) embankment's foundations were built but he had misgivings about the work's integrity. He frequently revisited the dam at his own expense after its completion in 1843, and was proven right: it leaked. However, his advice on repairs was shrugged aside by the commissioners, on grounds of cost.

The Night the Dam Burst

In early February 1852 torrential rain saw water levels reach record heights. Shortly after midnight, an 86 million gallon (391 million litre) wall of water burst down Digley Clough and onwards into the towns and villages of the Holme Valley, wreaking destruction and terror: entire mills, dye houses, rows of cottages and bridges were swept away. Coffins were even torn from graveyards and their contents washed into churches.

Many people fled to higher ground but 81 people lost their lives in the UK's fourth highest flood toll. Bodies were found months later, as far as 30 miles (48km) away. In the Digley and Holme valleys, where villages and towns had been humming with the vibrancy of the Industrial Revolution's peak, 7,000 people were put out of work. The disaster led to new laws dictating that only experienced and qualified engineers would be permitted to design dams.

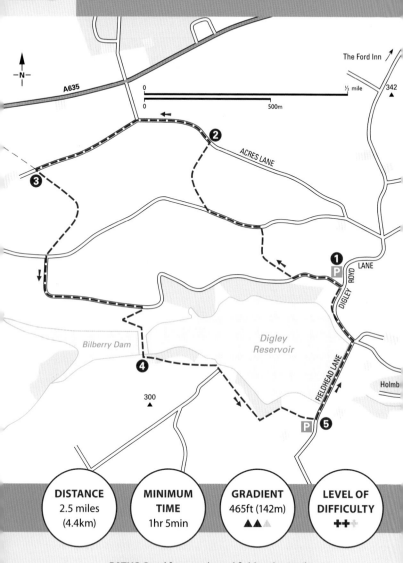

The Ford Inn

A635

ACRES LANE

DIGLEY ROYD LANE

FIELDHEAD LANE

Bilberry Dam

Digley Reservoir

Holmb

300

342

2
3
1 P
4
5 P

—N—

0 ½ mile
0 500m

DISTANCE	MINIMUM TIME	GRADIENT	LEVEL OF DIFFICULTY
2.5 miles (4.4km)	1hr 5min	465ft (142m) ▲▲▲	╋╋╋

PATHS Good farm tracks and field paths; 8 stiles
LANDSCAPE Pastures, intakes and reservoir sides
SUGGESTED MAP OS Explorer 288 Bradford & Huddersfield
START/FINISH Grid reference: SE 110072
DOG FRIENDLINESS Dogs should be on lead near livestock
PARKING Car park off Digley Royd Lane, Holmbridge
PUBLIC TOILETS None on route

WALK 28 DIRECTIONS

1 Take the ascending track to the side of the car park entrance. After 150yds (137m) take a path right, into an old quarried area. At a fork bear left, away from the quarry edge, soon swinging right up to a wooden stile. Ascend an enclosed path beyond to another stile. Cross that and continue for 20yds (18m), then turn left into a walled lane. The track forks after 250yds (229m); bear right, to a stile and into another walled lane. By an old quarry, 140yds (128m) later, the track becomes reedy but remains obvious and soon crosses a step stile into Acres Lane.

2 Turn left for 350yds (320m). When the road bends abruptly right, keep ahead over a stile by a metal gate and follow the lane beyond for 550yds (503m), to a crossroads of tracks.

3 Turn left, into another walled lane, winding down to a wooden stile and into a staggered crossroads of tracks. Keep ahead, descending to a bench

---

♿ ON THE WALK

You won't see any sign of the disaster on the walk, but in Holmfirth there's a memorial plaque to the dead on rebuilt Victoria Bridge, which had been demolished by the torrent. Elsewhere in the town, a memorial pillar for the 1801 Peace of Amiens also bears a plaque, at a height of about 7ft (2.1m), marking the level reached by the floodwaters.

---

where a sharp turn right, off this track, has you zig-zagging down to cross the rebuilt wall of Bilberry Dam.

4 Bear left up a path that's initially steep and bouldery, then sandy and well-defined. Pass through a redundant gate and swathes of bilberry and heather. Turn left through the next gate, on a purpose-built path. Through a second gate, turn left beyond a small stream, off the waymarked path, and on to Yorkshire Water's reservoir path. This contours easily across fields above the wooded reservoir edge. Beyond a third gate the path, now enclosed, heads through Digley South car park.

5 Turn left out of the car park, down Fieldhead Lane and across Digley Reservoir's wall to turn left along Back Top Lane, past the eight-arched flow chamber of Digley Reservoir. About 150yds (137m) beyond that, step off the road through a wooden gate on your left, to return to the car park via a short flight of steps, away from any traffic.

🍴 EATING AND DRINKING

Navvies and masons employed in the construction of Bilberry Dam often slaked their thirst at The Ford Inn. It stands on the moors above the reservoirs, at the junction of the Holmfirth to Greenhead A635 road and minor lanes between Meltham and Holmbridge. It serves light snacks in the day, good cooked meals in the evening and is family friendly.

Billberry Reservoir, scene of the 1852 dam disaster

SHIBDEN DALE

The estate from which a determined
woman defied convention.

On a hill above Halifax, Shibden Hall, a magnificent timbered-framed house, is set in 90 acres (36ha) of beautiful, rolling parkland. Dating from 1420, the hall has been owned by several prominent local families – the Oates, Saviles, Waterhouses and, latterly, the Listers. All left their mark on the fabric of the house but the original core remains intact and is now in the care of Calderdale Council, as a stunning museum.

Anne Lister – A Woman of Independent Means

The hall's most famous resident was Anne Lister, who lived there all her life, from 1791 to 1840. In 2010 her story won widespread renown when the BBC broadcast a drama based on her secret diaries and a documentary about her life. She was a wealthy landowner who had inherited Shibden Hall and its estates while in her mid-30s, and drew a reasonable income from tenancies which enabled her to remodel the house and to travel.

Anne defied society's stereotypical ideas of how a gentlewoman should behave. She was a fiercely independent industrialist, estate owner and traveller. While in the French Pyrénées in 1830, she became the first woman to scale Mont Perdu, and eight years later, with lover Ann Walker and local guide Henri Cazaux, did the first recorded tourist ascent of the Vignemale. To the French she became known as 'Lady Lister' but back home in Halifax she was sometimes referred to as 'Gentleman Jack' due to her openly lesbian lifestyle. She had celebrated a form of marriage to Walker, exceptionally unusual for the time, and Walker inherited the estate on Anne's death in 1840 while the two were travelling together in Georgia.

Anne's lifestyle was recorded in a diary kept for most of her life but wrote the most intimate accounts – around a sixth of the entries – in her own code, which wasn't cracked until the 1890s. To coincide with the BBC programmes, they were published as *The Secret Diaries of Miss Anne Lister*, edited by code translator Helena Whitbread.

This walk takes in the parkland that surrounds the hall, well-worth visiting, and ventures into the Shibden Valley, once part of Anne's extensive estate.

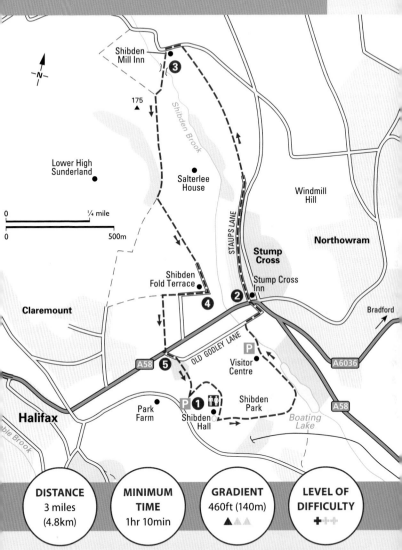

DISTANCE
3 miles
(4.8km)

MINIMUM TIME
1hr 10min

GRADIENT
460ft (140m)
▲▲△△

LEVEL OF DIFFICULTY
✚✚✚

PATHS Good tracks and field paths throughout; 1 stile **LANDSCAPE** Parkland, open fields and wooded valley **SUGGESTED MAP** OS Explorer 288 Bradford & Huddersfield **START/FINISH** Grid reference: SE 104257 **DOG FRIENDLINESS** Dogs can be exercised in Shibden Park but should otherwise be under close control **PARKING** Upper car park, Shibden Estate, off Shibden Old Road, Halifax. Car park closes at 5pm **PUBLIC TOILETS** At Shibden Hall, close to the start **NOTE** The busy A58 should be crossed with extreme caution, especially at peak periods. At Point ❷, use the pedestrian crossing 440yds (402m) to your left if necessary

WALK 29 DIRECTIONS

❶ Descend the gravel path from the car park to join a track running downhill. Follow signs for Shibden Mereside Visitor Centre, winding below Shibden Hall, past a lily pond and down a gravel track which ends near a play area. Head for the boating lake and walk along its edge. As you near the visitor centre turn right, through a car park, to a barrier. Cross the stream bridge beyond and head up the lane to a T-junction. Turn right, up Old Godley Lane, which eventually swings left up to the main road at Stump Cross.

❷ The busy A58 should be crossed with extreme caution, especially at peak periods. Use the pedestrian crossing 440yds (402m) to your left if necessary. After crossing, take Staups Lane, left of the Stump Cross Inn, on to cobbles. Where the cobbled lane forks stay right, to a junction. Go left and immediately left again down a track, which enters a field through a gate and follows a flagged track into Shibden Dale. Where this forks beyond a second wooden bench, bear left, and continue through a gate, to eventually emerge into a lane. Turn left to the Shibden Mill Inn and into the pub's car park.

❸ A track leaves the far end of the car park, crosses Shibden Brook (known as Red Beck) and ascends for 550yds (503m) to a fork. Bear left, slipping off the track on to a parallel flagged path to its left. While the track terminates in a yard, the path goes through a gate to cross a field diagonally, to a gap in its far wall, continuing along the field-edge beyond to a gate. Continue through a stile, into an enclosed path and through a yard. Follow a driveway, passing between cottages.

❹ Bear right, in front of Shibden Fold Terrace. Keep ahead when the driveway turns off left, scaling two steps into an enclosed path. At the far end, scale a gap in the wall and bear left, along a walled lane. Beyond two gates you pass farm buildings and drop to the A58. Turn down the pavement for 65yds (59m), and cross at the pedestrian crossing.

❺ Descend steps, cross Old Godley Lane and enter Shibden Park, following the vehicle track. At an information board the path, signed for Shibden Hall, takes off to the right, through a walling display back to the car park.

🍴 EATING AND DRINKING

Shibden Mill was first recorded in the early 1300s but it wasn't until 1890 that the successful Halifax brewery Samuel Webster & Sons transformed it into an inn. Tucked in a leafy corner of the dale, yet close to the centre of Halifax, this picturesque inn – today a free house – enjoys the best of both worlds. With a reputation for fine food and quality ales – including Shibden Bitter – the pub welcomes families. Well-behaved dogs can rest by the real fire in the bar.

HONLEY WOOD

Leave the noise of industry for peace and quiet among the trees.

Meltham's an industrious place. Set in its own small tributary valley of the River Holme, its large late-18th century Meltham Mills complex and neighbouring industrial areas still hum with activity. A few steps away from the mill, however, lies one of the largest areas of semi-natural ancient woodland in West Yorkshire.

Honley Wood

Honley Wood, beloved by locals for decades, is a 150-acre (60ha) expanse of upland oak and birch that offers immediate respite from and absolute contrast to the busy industries nearby.

The woods were quarried for many years and many of the rock outcrops you pass on this walk are old quarry faces, though nature has done such a good job reclaiming them that they appear completely natural. The woods remain in the ownership of a quarrying company but it has worked with the local authority and Holme Valley communities to improve access. Trails among the woods have been upgraded and the 7-mile (11.3km) Meltham Way cuts through the wood on its way round the valley.

In addition to the quarrying, evidence of coal extraction has also been found in the woods, along with prehistoric earthworks and burial sites dating back to the Bronze Age between 3,000 and 4,000 years ago.

The woods form part of the White Rose Forest, an initiative to improve and increase woodland cover and green spaces throughout the county while educating youngsters about the important relationship between the countryside and human activity. As you walk through the wood you'll occasionally be guided by White Rose Forest symbols.

Meltham's past industrial prosperity was based on Jonas Brook and Brothers' silk mill, established in the late 1800s, which employed 1,000 people in its prime. The Brooks provided their workers with housing and community buildings. The mills were taken over by David Brown Tractors in 1939 and grew to become Britain's largest post-war tractor manufacturer. The company continues today in Huddersfield, producing gear systems.

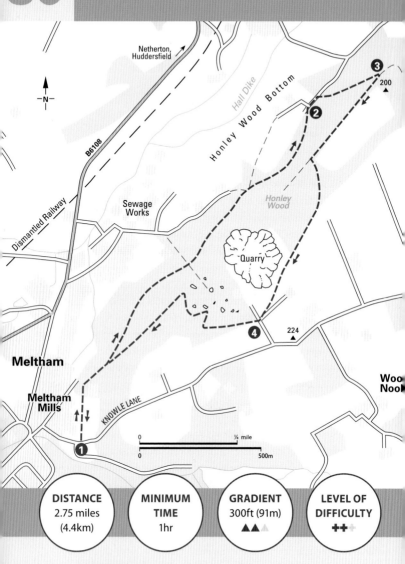

Netherton,
Huddersfield

Hall Dike

Honley Wood Bottom

B6108

Dismantled Railway

Sewage
Works

Honley
Wood

Quarry

Meltham

Meltham
Mills

KNOWLE LANE

**Woo
Noo**

200 ▲

224 ▲

❶ ❷ ❸ ❹

0 ¼ mile
0 500m

DISTANCE	MINIMUM TIME	GRADIENT	LEVEL OF DIFFICULTY
2.75 miles (4.4km)	1hr	300ft (91m) ▲▲▲	++✛

PATHS Woodland paths (some muddy) throughout; 1 stile
LANDSCAPE Peaceful woodland of oak, holly, rowan and more
SUGGESTED MAP OS Explorer 288 Bradford & Huddersfield
START/FINISH Grid reference: SE 109105
DOG FRIENDLINESS Plenty of opportunity for dogs to exercise
PARKING On-street parking around Knowle Lane, Meltham
PUBLIC TOILETS None on route

WALK 30 DIRECTIONS

❶ Pass between metal posts into the bridleway, close to the entrance of Link Business Park, walking between industrial areas to bear right into peaceful woodland. At the first fork bear left. Ignore minor paths to either side to pass springs before rising gently away from Meltham's industrial hum. Eventually the path drops to pass through another metal portal, into a walled track.

❷ In 60yds (55m) it meets a better-surfaced lane; continue ahead for 10yds (9m), then pass through a gap stile on your right signed 'Meltham Way'. This carries you back into the woods on a muddy, ascending path, topping out just beyond a large rock outcrop at a T-junction of paths.

❸ Turn right, along the level Meltham Way. Breaks in the trees allow occasional views across the Meltham Valley and beyond to distinctive Pule Hill, above Marsden, as well as Crosland Hall in the Colne Valley below, and the village of Netherton's church tower on the opposite valley side. The braided

> ### 🍂 ON THE WALK
> Unremarkable, flat earthen plinths, now overgrown and almost indistinguishable among the trees and shrubs on the woodland floor, are all that remain of charcoal hearths that once smouldered among the woods. Charcoal was an important fuel for iron smelting until it was superseded by coke during the Industrial Revolution.

path follows the fence on your left to fork right at the fence corner, with the Meltham Way across a wide track. Fork right immediately after, on an obvious track that follows a fence along the woodland to your right, joining another path met from the left. It now runs between a wall and a fence for 300yds (274m) to meet a lane, beyond a pair of large boulders.

❹ Cross the lane and pass through a metal portal opposite. Take the track ahead-left, which soon winds down into the woods on an engineered trail, past the outcrops of an old stone quarry. It descends to your outward path and back to the start point.

> ### 🍴 EATING AND DRINKING
> Just outside Meltham, on Blackmoorfoot Road, stands Will O' Nats, a freehouse with a dog-friendly bar and a popular restaurant. The pub is named after 1800s tenant William Dyson, son of Nathaniel Dyson. Though then called the Spotted Cow, locals knew it as Will O'Nats and the name stuck. When new owners renamed it the New House, in the early 1900s, a dray stopped in Meltham to ask directions but no-one had heard of the 'New House'. A quick change to 'Will O' Nats' ensured the beer didn't go astray again.

TO MERRYDALE

A reservoir circuit that takes you
to a popular picnic spot.

This easy stretch around Hill Top Reservoir above Slaithwaite in the Holme Valley is popular with local walkers and dog owners. The dam crossed early in the walk – also known as Slaithwaite Reservoir – was built across Merrydale Brook in 1796, one of several constructed in the Holme Valley to provide water for the Huddersfield Narrow Canal. The canal dams were built of earth with clay cores and 80 per cent of them leaked; many in Slaithwaite were conscious of the potential havoc to be wreaked if the dam failed and its 68.2 million gallons (310 million litres) spilled on to the town.

A Reservoir, a Waterfall and a Beauty Spot

The reservoir is especially popular with anglers, and is stocked with roach, bream, perch and carp. It has a reputation for being an excellent place to catch pike; the clough dammed to create the reservoir was steep-sided and the waters beneath its 11-acre (4.5ha) surface are deep, conditions favoured by large pike. Some anglers believe that large pike bite better after dusk, and night-time fishing is allowed on the reservoir. Fishing rights are held by Slaithwaite and District Angling Club and day tickets are available locally.

Further upstream is another body of water. The pond passed on the walk, near a fine waterfall, once served Clough House Mill, a huge woollen mill which later went over to cotton spinning. It was demolished in 1977, after almost two centuries of production. Its name lives on in nearby Clough House and Clough House Bridge. The mill is Schofield & Taylor vertical compound mill engine, named Elizabeth, has found a new home in Wortley Top Forge Industrial Museum at Thurgoland in South Yorkshire.

Upstream of the bridge is Merrydale, a beautiful clough that has been a popular countryside destination with locals for generations. Families employed in Slaithwaite's mills came here to walk, swim in the dams and picnic. It remains a quiet beauty spot to this day, looked after by the Friends of Merrydale and Kirklees Countryside Service. Though not on the route of this walk, it lies just a few paces upstream of the bridge crossed at the end of Point ❷ in the directions and is well worth the short diversion.

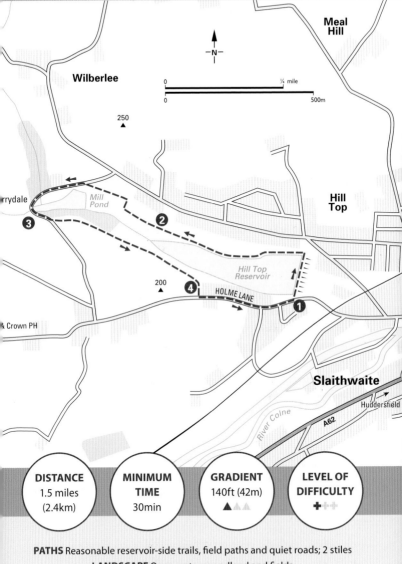

Meal Hill

Wilberlee

—N—

0 ¼ mile

0 500m

250 ▲

rrydale

Mill Pond

Hill Top

3

2

200 ▲

4

Hill Top Reservoir

HOLME LANE

1

& Crown PH

Slaithwaite

Huddersfield

River Colne

A62

DISTANCE	MINIMUM TIME	GRADIENT	LEVEL OF DIFFICULTY
1.5 miles (2.4km)	30min	140ft (42m) ▲△△	✚✚✚

PATHS Reasonable reservoir-side trails, field paths and quiet roads; 2 stiles

LANDSCAPE Open water, woodland and fields

SUGGESTED MAP OS Explorer OL21 South Pennines

START/FINISH Grid reference: SE 075140

DOG FRIENDLINESS Dogs can exercise freely around the reservoir

PARKING On-street parking around Holme Lane or in Slaithwaite itself

PUBLIC TOILETS None on route

WALK 31 DIRECTIONS

1 Take the footpath across Hill Top Reservoir's embankment. Turn left after crossing the spill channel, on a waterside path.

2 At the far end of the reservoir the path emerges from beneath trees into an open area. The path follows a brook upstream to a small section of wall, where it is spanned by a small weir. From there it veers right, up a rough track, past a pond to a road. Turn left, past a row of former weavers' cottages, over a bridge, following the road left.

3 After crossing a second bridge head up the road for 40yds (37m), then pass through a kissing gate on your left on to a path that carries you along the top of a 50ft (15m) retaining wall – don't look down – and is tight in places, where bushes have encroached. The noise of rushing water is the spill from the millpond below, passed earlier. Follow the fence-line path along the top edge of the woodland and over a stile, descending a little way towards the reservoir. Beyond another stile the path, now corralled between fences,

leads out of the trees on to a grassy path below fields and can be muddy.

4 At the far end, it slips between garden boundaries, and out on to Holme Lane. Turn left, downhill, back to the start.

> ### ⌛ IN THE AREA
> Slaithwaite's Moonraking Festival, described as a week of lanterns and legends – past festivals have featured alien hunts, storytelling and lantern processions – is held every other February. It's based on the legend that rascals caught with a rake by the canal bank tried to fob off customs men with the claim that they were raking in the moon, reflected on the water. In fact, they were retrieving barrels of smuggled brandy.

> ### 🐾 ON THE WALK
> Where the brook enters the reservoir you might catch sight of a grey heron. Herons are shy and will take to ungainly flight as you approach; their wingspan of more than 6ft (2m) is particularly impressive.

> ### 🍴 EATING AND DRINKING
> Offering commanding views across Merrydale, the Colne Valley and across the Holme Valley to Castle Hill, the Rose and Crown at Cop Hill is the perfect spot to reflect on your short walk over a meal and a refreshing brew. The free house is open all day, seven days a week, and welcomes families and well-behaved dogs. A children's menu is available, and the pub serves four real ales, including its own Cop Hill Best, brewed at the Goose Eye Brewery in Keighley.

FEATHERED VARIETY AT OGDEN WATER

Birds of moor, woodland and
water mix high above Halifax.

High on the moors just a few short miles from Halifax town centre, Ogden Water provides a surprisingly varied venue for rural walks. Waterside and woodland trails sit within a relatively small 148-acre (60ha) area, which is surrounded by a network of easily accessible wild moorland paths. The variety of landscape isn't just entertainment for walkers, it also provides superb habitat for a great diversity of birdlife.

A Countryside Retreat

Ogden has long been a countryside retreat for the people of Halifax. The 222 million gallon (1,010 million litre) dam was constructed between 1854 and 1857 to supply the town with water. The woodlands at the water's edge were planted in 1905 and it was declared a nature reserve in 2003.

More than 300,000 people visit Ogden Water annually, from dog walkers to weekend strollers and walking groups. Paths suitable for the disabled and pushchairs have been constructed around the reservoir and three permanent orienteering courses have been developed.

The 23-turbine power station that overlooks Ogden Water on Ovenden Moor was one of the first wind farms to be built in England. Its 103ft-high (31.5m) towers, at 1,411ft (430m) above sea level, are said by owner Yorkshire Windpower to produce energy for 5,000 homes, saving 10,396 tonnes of carbon dioxide emissions every year.

In summer the moor across which the spinning blades cast their shadows is home to red grouse, skylark and twite, while summer visitors include the curlew and the wheatear, so-called because of its conspicuous white rump. More unusual sightings in the area have included snow bunting, hen harrier and raven.

The woodlands surrounding the reservoir are also rich in birdlife – you might see goosanders, great crested grebe, sandpipers and goldeneye ducks on and around the water, as well as woodpeckers among the trees. Flocks of crossbills have been known to feed among the larch and conifers and short-eared owls roost in the trees near the moor.

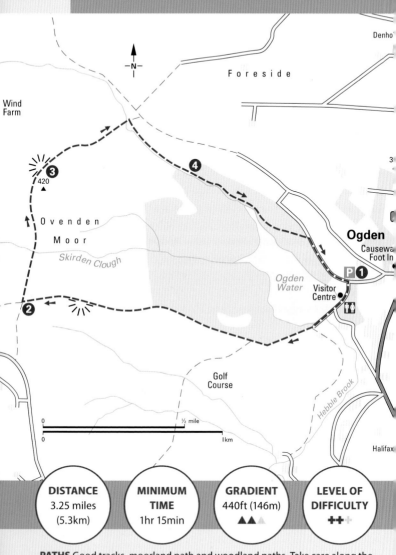

WALK 32 DIRECTIONS

❶ From the welcome board by the disabled parking area, head down the surfaced lane, past Ogden Water Visitor Centre and the toilet block. Cross the dam wall and continue up the concrete track ahead, between a golf course on your left and the woodland over the wall to your right. The building on the horizon ahead was once The Withens Hotel and, standing at 1,408ft (429m) above sea level, was regarded as West Yorkshire's highest pub until it closed in 2001 following a fire. It is now a private residence. Ignore paths off to either side, as the view to the left expands to include Mixenden Reservoir, and across to Halifax where Wainhouse Tower is prominent. The ascending track passes through a metal gate and Ovenden Moor Wind Farm soon comes into view.

❷ About 1.5 miles (2.4km) beyond the dam, just as the track veers gently left toward the former pub, turn right, through a kissing gate, on to a well-worn footpath across Ovenden Moor. It seems strange to have such a view from a bleak Pennine moor, while immediately right is the intense urban spread of the city of Bradford. The path dips across a silt trap in Skirden Clough, then rises again to top-out by a large cairn, from which the views extend across to Rombald's Moor, north of Bradford, and beyond that Blubberhouses Moor on the southern edge of the Yorkshire Dales.

❸ As it descends the path, occasionally marked by cairns and wooden posts, widens and becomes muddier. It crosses a second clough, with another silt trap. Don't climb the stone steps on the opposite bank. Instead turn right, on a signed permissive path provided by Yorkshire Water to Ogden Water. This uneven way descends further into the clough past a series of small waterfalls. Ignore the two footbridges on your left and follow the stream to the woodland edge.

❹ Enter the woodland through a stile and follow the streamside path. Its bouldery surface soon gives way to gravel, and winds away from the stream. Ignore a path to the right and keep ahead, heading left at the next fork. Keep left at a second fork, above a small footbridge and pond. The path climbs gently to a metal gate. Pass through the stile to its left, and turn right along a walled track, past a dry-stone walling display area, back into the car park.

🍴 EATING AND DRINKING

A visitor centre, staffed by volunteer members of the Friends of Ogden Water, offers light refreshments, as well as books, maps and confectionary. When it's closed, the Causeway Foot Inn, at the end of Ogden Lane by the busy A629, welcomes families and their dogs alike. Open Wednesday to Sunday, the traditional menu often features seasonal game.

NORLAND MOOR'S SACRIFICIAL PAST

Grand views across the Calder Valley
from a moorland plateau.

Norland Moor is close to the start of the Calderdale Way, a 50-mile (80km) circuit of the borough of Calderdale which, when it opened in October 1978, was Britain's first Recreational Trail. There are panoramic views straight away, as the waymarked walk accompanies the edge of Norland Moor. The route was inaugurated to link some of the best Pennine landscapes and historical sites – moors, mills, gritstone outcrops, wooded cloughs, hand-weaving hamlets and industrial towns – into an invigorating walk while bringing economic benefits to local communities along its route.

Views and Carvings Across the Moors

Norland Moor is a 253-acre (102ha) tract of heather moorland overlooking Sowerby Bridge and both the Calder and Ryburn valleys. Criss-crossed by paths, it is popular with local walkers. Riven by old quarry workings, it is a reminder that here in West Yorkshire you are seldom far from a site of industry. Originally a part of the Savile estates, the moor was bought for £250 after a public appeal in 1932. It still has the status of a common. Part of the attraction is to find such splendid walking country so close to the busy towns in the valley.

Ladstone Rock is a gritstone outcrop with a distinctive profile that stares out over the Ryburn Valley from the edge of Norland Moor. If you can believe the stories, barbaric human sacrifices were carried out on the rock by blood-thirsty druids, and convicted witches were thrown off it. The name might have Celtic roots, meaning to cut or to kill.

There is a tradition in the South Pennines of carving inspirational quotations into such rocks. Ladstone Rock (Point ❷) among the names, dates and expressions of undying love, is a small metal plaque inscribed with a short psalm from the Bible.

During the walk you get good views from the moor across the valley to Sowerby Bridge and the outskirts of Halifax. Dominating the view is a curious edifice known as Wainhouse Tower, which is opened up to the public on just a few occasions each year – generally on bank holidays.

Opposite: Wainhouse Tower

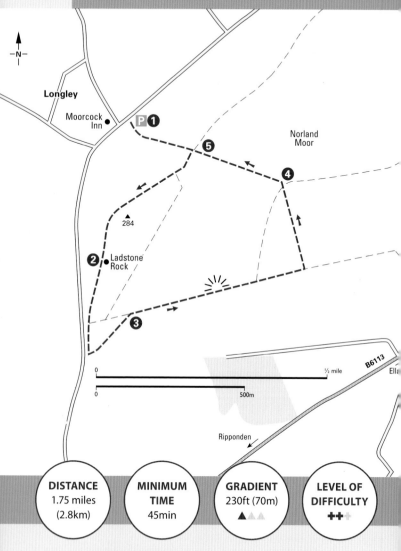

<table>
<tr><td>DISTANCE
1.75 miles
(2.8km)</td><td>MINIMUM TIME
45min</td><td>GRADIENT
230ft (70m)
▲▲▲</td><td>LEVEL OF DIFFICULTY
✦✦✦</td></tr>
</table>

PATHS Good moorland paths and tracks; no stiles
LANDSCAPE Heather moor and regenerative woodland
SUGGESTED MAP OS Explorer OL21 South Pennines
START/FINISH Grid reference: SE 055217
DOG FRIENDLINESS Dogs can roam off lead unless there are grazing sheep
PARKING Small car park opposite the Moorcock Inn on Moor Bottom Lane,
Norland Moor **PUBLIC TOILETS** None on route

WALK 33 DIRECTIONS

❶ Leave the car park on the well-used path that leads from the Access Land information board, away from the Moorcock Inn. Bear right at two successive forks as you climb, until you reach the moor-edge path, among heather and bilberry, high above the Moorcock Inn. Enjoy expansive views across the Calder Valley as you pass the gritstone outcrop known as Ladstone Rock.

❷ Keep straight ahead, now on a more substantial track, which descends to run beside the road. Reaching the corner of a wall by a caravan site turn left, alongside the wall, for a few strides. Where a bridleway passes through a metal gate ahead, disregard it and instead bear gently left, on a path that cuts a jinking line up the moor to a wall corner.

❸ Continue ahead, now with the wall on your right, into an area of silver birch. At a junction, 500yds (457m) after meeting the wall, turn left along a walled track, between fields on your right and birch woodland on your left. Ahead to your right,

Wainhouse Tower rises above far away Halifax, while the blades of Ovenden Moor wind farm's turbines turn relentlessly ahead.

> 🍴 **EATING AND DRINKING**
> Your best choice is the Moorcock Inn, opposite the car park. This is a popular meeting place for local walking and rambling clubs – either before their walk or after. It offers freshly cooked meals and a children's menu. It also serves Yorkshire-brewed cask ales.

❹ Follow the track to a wall corner, where three options present themselves. Take the middle route, ahead-left, which crosses the heart of the heath to reach the moor-edge path by a small, overgrown delph, or stone quarry. Take the path to its left, indicated by a wooden post and, where it forks after a few strides, bear down left, to a second marker.

❺ Turn right here, as directed by the waymarker, then keep left on the path soon joined, which drops back to the car park.

> 🌿 **IN THE AREA**
> After years of dereliction, the canal marina in Sowerby Bridge has been brought back to life. The centre of town was closed off to traffic for almost a year, while a filled-in section of canal was opened up to boats once again. This was made possible by building what is now – at almost 20ft (6m) – the deepest canal lock in the country.

TUNNEL END

Explore the landscape above Marsden,
then visit Britain's longest canal tunnel.

When Standedge Tunnel was dug to carry the Huddersfield Narrow Canal under the Pennines between 1794 and 1811, it was built without a tow path, which would have required a wider, more expensive bore. The horses that drew the unpowered barges therefore had to be unhitched and led from Marsden, over Standedge Moor to Diggle, ready to continue the journey.

The boats, meanwhile, were 'legged' through the tunnel. Men would lie either on their backs on the boat's roof or on a plank across its bow and propel the boat along by pressing their feet against the roof or sides – effectively walking on the ceiling or along the walls.

Life on the Canal

In smaller canal tunnels this was easily handled by the boat's crew but in Standedge it was no small feat. At 3.25 miles (5.3km) long it is Britain's longest canal tunnel. The leggers here were professionals and a team of experts could get an unladen craft through in 80 minutes – little more than it would take a strong walker to cover the same distance above ground – while a laden boat might take three hours. For that they earned a shilling and sixpence – worth seven and a half pence in new money.

Four passing places had been built in the tunnel but as traffic grew bottlenecks developed and fights ensued as crews refused to give way to boats from the opposite direction. In response, the canal company insisted that boats use their own leggers, and introduced a traffic management system. A convoy would enter the tunnel at one end and a chain was fastened across the entrance after the last boat. The horses, together with the bargees' children, would be led over the moor by a company employee who would unchain the other end in time for the convoy to emerge. The return journey of around 7 miles (11.3km) would be undertaken at least twice a day.

Though the canal had opened in 1799, it was another 12 years before the tunnel was ready, but before long the railways had seen off much of the canal business. The Huddersfield Narrow Canal closed in 1943 and its tunnel locked in 1951. Both have since been restored to cater for the leisure trade.

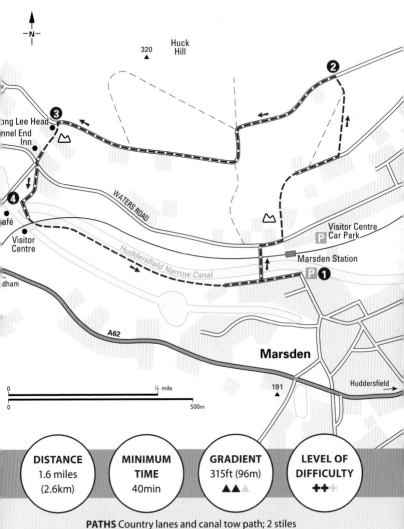

DISTANCE	MINIMUM TIME	GRADIENT	LEVEL OF DIFFICULTY
1.6 miles (2.6km)	40min	315ft (96m) ▲▲△	++

PATHS Country lanes and canal tow path; 2 stiles
LANDSCAPE Valley-side tracks and waterways, with views to peaty uplands
SUGGESTED MAP OS Explorer OL21 South Pennines
START/FINISH Grid reference: SE 047118
DOG FRIENDLINESS Dogs should be under close control throughout
PARKING Standedge Tunnel car park, by Marsden Railway Station
PUBLIC TOILETS At the visitor centre along the route; disabled toilets are at Tunnel End's café

WALK 34 DIRECTIONS

1 Leave the car park and cross the road bridge spanning the canal and railway. Turn right and after 50yds (46m) take Spring Head Lane steeply up to a white-painted house. Bear right, between yellow metal posts, along a grassy path. After a few paces this meets a driveway; turn left over a stile to ascend a walled lane. Just beyond the point at which another path joins yours from the left, the lane reaches a T-junction.

2 Turn left along a rough lane, between farm buildings. Beyond, the lane offers excellent views. Bear left at a junction, down the Kirklees Way, on a track which soon swings right to pass two farms.

IN THE AREA

To appreciate the work of the leggers, you couldn't do much better than take a three-hour trip through Standedge Tunnel. British Waterways operates boat trips through the tunnel, from the visitor centre at Tunnel End to Diggle, on the first Saturday of every month. For details contact 01782 785703 or visit www. standedge.co.uk.

🍴 EATING AND DRINKING

Tunnel End Inn has been quenching thirsts for more than two centuries, initially as an alehouse serving the navvies building the Huddersfield Narrow Canal and Standedge Tunnel. The original farm building that had stood on the site for a century was rebuilt as a pub in 1850 and today welcomes dozens of passing walkers and their dogs, offering four real ales and renowned homemade meals.

3 Just before a house named Tong Lee Head, turn left, through a gate in the wall and down a steep grassy path. It crosses a private lawn and descends steps by a house before crossing a stile, emerging next to the Tunnel End Inn. Cross Waters Road into the grounds of the Standedge Tunnel Visitor Centre.

4 Join the Huddersfield Narrow Canal's tow path from the disabled parking area within the visitor centre grounds, crossing the canal on a short bridge before dropping to the tow path, signed towards Marsden. When you reach Lock 42 East, 0.5 miles later (800m), you're back at the start.

🥾 ON THE WALK

If you're returning to Marsden along the canal tow path in spring, keep an eye out for toads. In the breeding season, thousands migrate simultaneously from their wintertime hibernation places back to the ponds in which they were born to spawn, usually after sunset. Marsden's old mill ponds and mill leats make excellent breeding spots for toads.

WADE WOODS AND THE CAT I'TH WELL

One of West Yorkshire's most beautiful, tranquil valleys.

Luddenden Dean is a tranquil gem, tucked away in a corner of Calderdale with only limited road access. Despite the valley's small population its remote Cat i'th Well pub is rarely quiet.

A Site of Scientific Interest and a Private Estate

Jerusalem Farm itself is a 32-acre (13ha) nature reserve set in a valley carved out by a glacier some 30,000 years ago. The converted farm buildings offer facilities to school groups, and Calderdale Council's Countryside Service runs environmental education workshops, providing an eclectic mixture of subjects, from mankind's effects on the landscape to environmental art.

The farm has its own, tents-only campsite, sited above Wade Wood, a Site of Special Scientific Interest. Among its many trees and plants are species that suggest this could be ancient woodland, looking much as it would have in the wake of the last ice age 12,000 years ago.

At the valley head stands an ornate gateway, the entrance to the old Castle Carr Estate. There are no public rights of way through the estate, though guided walks led by ramblers, or local walking festival events, are occasionally granted permission to enter the grounds.

The estate was established by Captain Joseph Priestley Edwards in the mid-1800s. After buying up large areas of farm and moorland, he set about building a mansion of breathtaking opulence. Mile-long driveways led to a coach house for half a dozen carriages. Beyond a Norman archway – complete with portcullis – was a huge banqueting hall with an oak-framed ceiling and a floor laid on springs for dancing.

The grounds were even more impressive: laid out around a series of reservoirs, their focal point was five fountains, the highest of which flung water 130ft (40m) into the air – said to be the highest in Europe.

Edwards died in a railway disaster in Abergele in 1868, before the house was finished. Successive owners found the estate too expensive to maintain and the house was demolished in the 1960s. The ornate fountains are occasionally brought back to life, as great a spectacle today as they ever were.

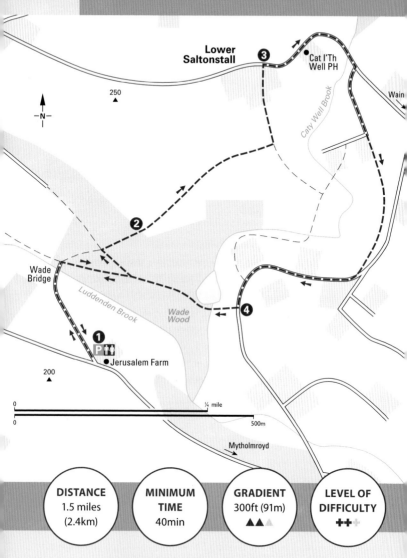

DISTANCE
1.5 miles
(2.4km)

MINIMUM
TIME
40min

GRADIENT
300ft (91m)
▲▲▲

LEVEL OF
DIFFICULTY
+++

PATHS Wood and field paths, quiet lanes; 3 stiles
LANDSCAPE Valley bottom woodland and cobbled lanes
SUGGESTED MAP OS Explorer OL21 South Pennines
START/FINISH Grid reference: SE 036278
DOG FRIENDLINESS Dogs should be on lead when not in the woodland
PARKING Jerusalem Farm car park, Luddenden Dean, open between 8.30am
and 6pm **PUBLIC TOILETS** Campsite toilets at Jerusalem Farm

WALK 35 DIRECTIONS

❶ Pass through the stile at the bottom of the car park and descend the walled lane beyond, to cross Wade Bridge over Luddenden Brook. Several routes diverge from the opposite bank: take the broad, timber-edged path which climbs gently ahead-right. At a junction, bear left on the ascending Calderdale Way. At a second junction, head up steps to your right, signed 'Saltonstall', into a well-worn earthy path that ascends to a gate through a fence in a field corner. Through this bear slightly right for 20yds (18m) to climb a stile, being careful not to dislodge loose wall stones.

❷ Cross the next field diagonally to its top-right corner. Pass through the gate there and maintain direction across the next field, to pass through an open gateway. Parallel the top-left wall through the next field to a wooden gate in its top corner. After that and the stile beyond turn left, ascending the final field, to exit through a small gate in the top-left corner. Ascend a rough driveway to a metalled road.

> ### 🌱 IN THE AREA
> Clogs – the footwear worn by the thousands of people who worked in West Yorkshire's mills – are still produced in Calderdale. Walkey Clogs, of Mount Pleasant Mills, Mytholmroyd, is the last place where British clogs are entirely hand-made.

❸ Turn right, down the quiet lane, past the Cat I'Th Well pub. Cross Caty Well Bridge over Caty Well Brook and climb the lane for 60yds (55m), to take a surfaced track off to the right signed 'Public Footpath'. Through a wooden gate at the end pass to the left of a cottage and take a gate beyond a strip of grass. Bear right on a 330yd (302m) field-edge path and back into the lane at its far end. Turn right, downhill, past a row of cottages known as Jowler.

❹ In 90yds (82m) beyond the cottages, where a sign points to Jerusalem Farm, pass through a gap in the wall on your right and descend steps, kinking left at the bottom on a cinder track for 10yds (9m), then right, down more steps. Pass through a kissing gate and cross a bridge over the outflow of a small pond. Around 100yds (91m) past an area of woodland art, the path forks. Bear left, descending your outward path back to Wade Bridge and the track to the car park.

> ### 🍴 EATING AND DRINKING
> Pictures on the walls in the Cat I'Th Well pub show life at Castle Carr, the large estate at the valley head, in the days before its demolition. The pub serves food at weekends (and pie and peas on Wednesday evenings) and offers child-size portions as well as adult ones. Dogs are welcome in the bar and beer garden. Three Timothy Taylor cask ales are served, along with three rotating guest beers.

WORTH VALLEY AND THE RAILWAY CHILDREN

Relive the days of steam
between Oxenhope and Haworth.

The Keighley and Worth Valley Railway is one of the most scenic preserved steam operations in England. So much so that, in 1970, when Lionel Jeffries was looking for a location for his directorial debut *The Railway Children*, he chose the Worth Valley. The film, which starred Bernard Cribbins and gave young actresses Jenny Agutter and Sally Thomsett each their first taste of fame, is regarded a classic family movie.

An All-time Classic

At the time the movie was made, the line had been run by volunteers for a mere two years. It was built in 1867 by Haworth mill owners to transport their goods down the valley to link with the Midland Railway at Keighley, for national distribution. Oxenhope's own mill owners paid for it to be extended 1.5 miles (2.4km) to their woollen factories and the line was sold to the Midland, keen to stave off competition from the Great Northern. Following nationalisation after the Second World War, the branch line was closed by British Rail in 1962 and sold to the preservation society six years later.

Today the line, along which services operate year-round, is the only fully preserved branch line in England. This walk follows the short extension between Oxenhope and Haworth, following Bridgehouse Beck downstream. Along the way you will pass long-overgrown millponds and 19th-century goits – man-made water channels – built to raise the head of water to power waterwheels in the mills of Haworth.

Haworth itself is famous not only for the railway but also for the sisters Anne, Emily and Charlotte, the famous Brontë novelists, who resided with their preacher father at Haworth Parsonage in the mid-1800s. The Parsonage is now a museum run by the Brontë Society, full of family memorabilia and original furniture. Novels such as Charlotte's *Jane Eyre*, Anne's *The Tenant of Wildfell Hall* and Emily's *Wuthering Heights* were written here and it's become a destination for hundreds of thousands of literary pilgrims every year. Less well-known is the fact that the Parsonage also served as the location for Doctor Forrest's surgery in *The Railway Children* movie.

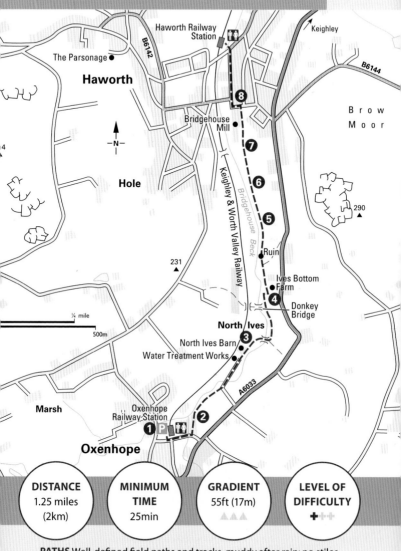

DISTANCE	MINIMUM TIME	GRADIENT	LEVEL OF DIFFICULTY
1.25 miles (2km)	25min	55ft (17m) ▲▲▲	✚✚✚

PATHS Well-defined field paths and tracks, muddy after rain; no stiles
LANDSCAPE Valley bottom fields overlooked by moorland edges
SUGGESTED MAP OS Explorer OL21 South Pennines **START/FINISH** Grid
reference: SE 032353 **DOG FRIENDLINESS** On lead beyond Ives Bottom Farm
PARKING Free car park at Oxenhope station **PUBLIC TOILETS** Oxenhope
and Haworth stations **NOTE** Allow extra time for the return rail journey, and
remember to take money for the fare. Weekend services run year-round but
weekdays are seasonal. Visit www.kwvr.co.uk or call 01535 647777 for a timetable

Walk
36
Oxenhope

WALK 36 DIRECTIONS

1 Leave the car park and turn left into Mill Lane. After 150yds (137m) turn left, on a bridleway signed as the Worth and Brontë Ways. The surfaced section ends after just a few paces, as you pass the station's overflow car park, and a narrower path continues through a gap between a wall and a metal field gate.

2 The field-edge path follows Bridgehouse Beck downstream for 250yds (229m) before crossing a footbridge to the opposite bank and turning right down a walled path between the railway and the stream. A gate soon leads out on to a lane past Oxenhope water treatment works.

3 Beyond North Ives Barn, the path goes through a gap in the wall ahead and past a small fenced pond, crosses a second metal footbridge. Turning left, downstream, along the edges of three fields, you pass the stone Donkey Bridge. The path braids in places but the different trails meet again and soon head into trees, emerging for a brief climb, by a bramble-choked fence, to the driveway of Ives Bottom Farm.

4 Turn left through the farmyard, then left again at a fork in the track beyond. Through a small latched gate, the path leads to a flight of steps through a wall and passes a ruined house. Follow the fence on your left across the next field, ignoring the stream-bound path that crosses your route.

5 Beyond a kissing gate, the path enters a stand of trees around a former mill pond. Stay on the path following the course of the water channel.

6 A small footbridge on your right at the far end of the overgrown ponds leads to a kissing gate, beyond which you turn left along the braided field-edge path, past a spring flowing into a stone trough, to another kissing gate beneath a large beech tree.

> ### 🍴 EATING AND DRINKING
> Since 1982, the former British Rail buffet car at Oxenhope Station has served simple fare including soup, sandwiches, pies and pasties. Open weekends between 9am and 3.30pm, and occasional weekdays (call 01535 645214 to check first).

7 A wider, grassy lane leads to a kissing gate below a pigeon loft. Through this, bear immediately right, then left, and follow fences to a latched metal gate. The path now runs between a wall and a fence for 80yds (73m) before descending stone steps next to Bridgehouse Mill, into Brow Road in Haworth.

8 A few dozen downhill strides bring you to a junction. Turn left, over the railway bridge and up Bridgehouse Lane for Haworth or right along Station Road for the railway station, seen across the road, and a steam train back to Oxenhope.

THE GRITSTONE CRAGS OF THE WESTERN MOORS

Walk around West Yorkshire's most beautifully located body of water.

Of all the moorland reservoirs that stud West Yorkshire's peaty uplands, Widddop is the shining jewel, a glittering pool set in a wide, crag-rimmed hollow surrounded by mile-after-mile of rolling peaty moorland. Poet Laureate Ted Hughes, who was born just a few miles away in Mytholmroyd in 1930, described it as a 'frightened lake' in *Remains of Elmet*, the famous volume of poems about his vanishing South Pennine boyhood.

Widddop was, between 1871 and 1878, the first of the reservoirs to be built on the moors above Heptonstall to supply drinking water to Halifax. With a capacity of 633 million gallons (2,878 million litres) it's also the largest.

During construction a small, temporary village of wooden huts, with its own bake house and store, was built at Widddop. Locals nicknamed it 'Navvyopolis' and around 200 men lived there when construction was at its peak. Materials for the dam that couldn't be found on site were brought along a horse-drawn tramway which ran from Shackleton, above the National Trust's main car park at Hardcastle Crags, along the edge of the Hebden Valley to Holme End, Clough Foot and then Widddop. Materials were pulled up the hillside to Shackleton by a stationary engine on an inclined tramway, the huge ramp for which can be seen in the lower reaches of Crimsworth Dean. The tramline can still be traced on foot from Shackleton.

The Cludders

The impressive gritstone crags that frame the southern edge of the reservoir so picturesquely are The Cludders, more commonly known as Widddop Rocks. They're very popular with climbers; renowned climber Don Whillans did the first ascent of a route known as Ceiling Crack here in 1955. Other rocks near by have equally evocative names: Clattering Stones, Boggart Stones, Slack Stones and Frock Holes.

The boulders scattered beneath Cludders have also attracted others. John Wesley, the Methodist preacher, is said to have delivered a sermon to Widddop's isolated population from one of them in 1766 – one is inscribed with his initials and the date.

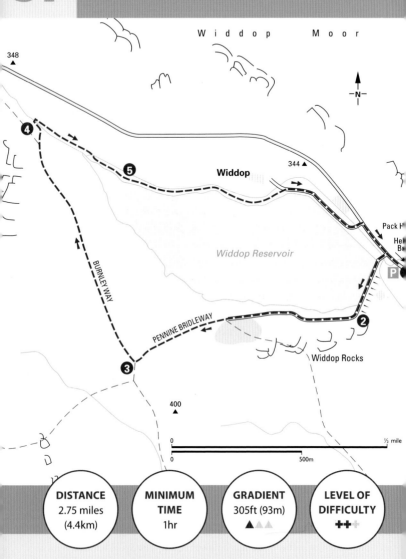

DISTANCE	MINIMUM TIME	GRADIENT	LEVEL OF DIFFICULTY
2.75 miles (4.4km)	1hr	305ft (93m) ▲▲▲	++✛

PATHS Good tracks and paths, some potentially boggy moorland; no stiles
LANDSCAPE Reservoir set in crag-surrounded moorland bowl
SUGGESTED MAP OS Explorer OL21 South Pennines
START/FINISH Grid reference: SD 937327
DOG FRIENDLINESS Sheep graze the moors around Widdop so dogs
should be on lead or under close control **PARKING** Widdop Reservoir car park,
Widdop, near Hebden Bridge **PUBLIC TOILETS** None on route

WALK 37 DIRECTIONS

❶ A gap in the car park wall, next to the information boards, puts you on a short, grassy path towards the reservoir wall. Cross a metal footbridge over the dam's spill channel and turn left to cross the embankment.

❷ Bear right at the end of the dam wall, along a track known as Gorple Gate, actually an old packhorse route that climbs from Worsthorne to Heptonstall. After passing a small plantation the trail climbs gently away from the reservoir up a small clough and bears right, across the small stream near the top.

❸ At a junction just above you'll find a Burnley Way marker post; turn right on a rough path, which can be muddy.

❹ Leave Burnley Way at the foot of the path, where a fingerpost directs you back towards the dam, over a footbridge to a second fingerpost; bear right. By a silt trap pond, where Old Hay Dyke's waters flow into the dam, the path runs to the right of a wall for a few paces, then carries you over another footbridge and turns left, between the water course and the reservoir.

❺ Continue along the path past the former reservoir keeper's house on your left. Cross the water course on a short vehicle track, which leads, through a metal gate, on to the road. Turn right down the tarmac for a short distance to return to the car park.

LUMB FALLS AND LIMERS GATE

The forgotten valley of Crimsworth Dean
and an exquisite packhorse bridge.

West Yorkshire might be rich in the kind of quarried sandstones that form the foundations of the Houses of Parliament and pave Trafalgar Square in London. Naturally occurring lime however, an important mineral for agriculture and building, is in short supply and for centuries has been imported into the county.

Limers Gate, which crosses Crimsworth Dean near Hebden Bridge, is a centuries-old packhorse route. The word 'gate' is derived from the middle-English term 'geat', for road or path, while 'lime' is a clue as to what cargo was borne along it by packhorse trains.

In the days before turnpike roads and the Industrial Revolution, travellers kept to the higher ground, which allowed easier travel than the damp valley bottoms. Limers Gate started in limestone country, in Lothersdale, near Skipton, and crossed the high moors above Wycoller and Walshaw Dean before dropping to Lumb Falls in Crimsworth Dean. It then rose again, on to Wadsworth Moor and the heights above Luddenden Dean, towards its final destination in Halifax.

Above Lumb Falls a packhorse bridge spans Crimsworth Dean Beck above a waterfall which, when frozen in a hard winter, resembles the pipes of a giant church organ. Though its sides are now fenced, these would have impeded the progress of the ponies laden with bulging panniers.

A Site of Scientific Interest

The small dell in which the bridge and falls sit is classified as a geological Site of Special Scientific Interest. The lip of the waterfall is Lower Kinderscout gristone, while the rock beneath is a softer mudstone, hence its slight overhang. Shales beneath the falls have been eroded to form a pool, popular with picnickers and wild swimmers though it's too shallow to allow diving.

Wildlife thrives here – kestrels hover above surrounding fields, and heron and grey wagtail can be seen around the falls – while the idyllic scene is credited with having inspired the late poet laureate Ted Hughes, born just a few miles away in Mytholmroyd, to put pen to paper.

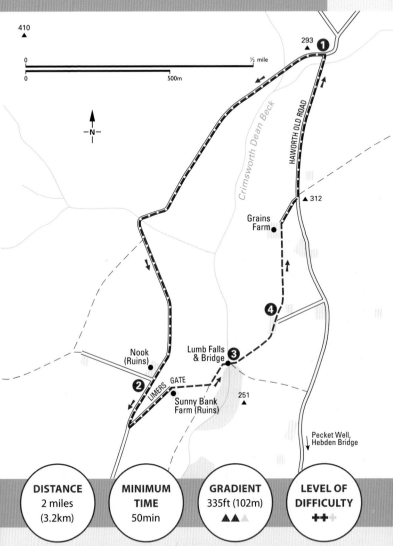

410 ▲

293 ▲ ❶

0
½ mile
0
500m

—N—

Crimsworth Dean Beck

HAWORTH OLD ROAD

▲ 312

Grains
Farm ●

❹

Nook
(Ruins)

Lumb Falls
& Bridge ❸

❷ LIMERS GATE

Sunny Bank
Farm (Ruins) ●

251 ▲

Pecket Well,
↓ Hebden Bridge

DISTANCE	MINIMUM TIME	GRADIENT	LEVEL OF DIFFICULTY
2 miles (3.2km)	50min	335ft (102m) ▲▲▲	✚✚✚

PATHS Good tracks and field paths; 3 stiles **LANDSCAPE** Gritty Pennine valley
with wooded sides and extensive views **SUGGESTED MAP** OS Explorer OL21
South Pennines **START/FINISH** Grid reference: SD 996324
DOG FRIENDLINESS Livestock grazes along the route so dogs should be under
close control or on lead at all times **PARKING** Quite limited at Grain Water Bridge,
on Haworth Old Road. Park considerately, without blocking the lane or any field
gates **PUBLIC TOILETS** None on route **NOTE** The start is near the end of a narrow
lane with few passing places

WALK 38 DIRECTIONS

1 Take the bridleway signed 'Aire Link, Pennine Bridleway', that follows Crimsworth Dean Beck gently downstream, soon passing through a latched wooden gate to cross a second beck near the confluence of the two. For the next 1,000yds (914m) the track rises gently. The track passes a collapsed farm building and, 550yds (503m) later, crosses the muddy yard of an abandoned farm known as Nook.

2 Keep ahead at the trail junction immediately beyond the farm. After 150yds (137m) bear sharp left, doubling back on a walled grassy bridleway signed for Lumb Bridge. This is Limers Gate, the ancient packhorse route, and in places is obstructed by dense reeds and running water but you can easily step off to the right, and follow it down on drier ground past the skeletal remains of Sunny Bank Farm. Firmer and clearer ground soon appears in the lane though care should be taken on grass-covered boulders. The lane drops to Lumb Falls, crossing Crimsworth Dean Beck on the ancient packhorse bridge.

3 On the opposite bank, leave Limers Gate by stepping over the stile on your left, then bearing right into an enclosed flight of stone steps. Emerging into an open field, continue uphill to another stile. Keep ahead beyond, up a pair of steps, then gently bear left to pass through a wooden gate and across a farm courtyard. Take the clearly marked path between barns, scaling a few steps beyond, to a latched gate.

4 Cross the field ahead, aiming for the lower of two farmhouses. Beyond the stile through the far wall keep ahead, aiming for the far bottom field corner. Pass through a gate here and bear right on a flagged wallside path to a gate into the yard of Grains Farm. Ascend the surfaced driveway then turn left to return to the start point.

> ### 🦅 ON THE WALK
> Dippers seem to love the waterfalls below Lumb Bridge and can often be seen whirring up-and-down the beck or stood on the falls' rim, bobbing up and down.

> ### 🍴 EATING AND DRINKING
> 'If Robin Hood be not at home, come take a pot with little John.' So reads the old sign above the door of the Robin Hood Inn, a former coach house which stands at Pecket Well, on the A6033 former turnpike road between Hebden Bridge and Haworth. The pub offers a full menu lunchtimes, evenings and all day at weekends, with options for children and pensioners. Four cask ales are offered and dogs are welcome in the bar area.

GIBSON MILL AND SLURRING ROCK

Yesterday's theme park,
tomorrow's technology.

Hebden Dale, down which peaty brown Hebden Water cascades over boulders, through thick stands of oak, beech, Scots pine, ash and more, is one of the most outstanding wooded valleys in the country. It's long been a favourite destination for walkers, who used to arrive by steam train from mill towns across West Yorkshire and Lancashire, alighting in Hebden Bridge for the charabanc ride up the delightful valley.

Gibson Mill stands at the heart of the beautiful woodland. Built in 1800, as the Industrial Revolution began to gather steam, the mill produced cotton cloth for the best part of a century – the damp, valley bottom site was ideal as the humidity helped prevent the highly flammable raw cotton fibres from combusting – before the development of the canal and railway network saw production move to more accessible towns such as nearby Hebden Bridge.

A New Lease of Life
The mill then found new life as a pleasure ground, offering roller skating, dining on the upper floors and dance nights for youngsters, who would walk miles for the chance of perhaps meeting the love of their life. Stands selling mineral waters sprang up in the mill yard, swing boats operated nearby and several pavilions provided refreshments. Today the site is so peaceful that it's difficult to appreciate the mill's popularity – at its peak, before the Second World War, the dining hall could cater for as many as 500 diners.

Since the 1950s, the mill and much of the surrounding woodland have been in the care of the National Trust. For years the building was used variously as a scout base and a tool store for the estate. In the 1990s the trust decided to create a café and visitor centre and, with the mill being too remote for services such as piped water, sewerage and electricity, it employed green architects Eco Arc to design a sustainable solution. Today the mill's café and visitor centre are entirely self-sufficient in energy and water, with dry composting toilets, electricity from solar power panels on the roof, a biomass boiler fuelled from the surrounding woodlands and a spring water supply. The ancient mill now works in harmony with the surrounding landscape.

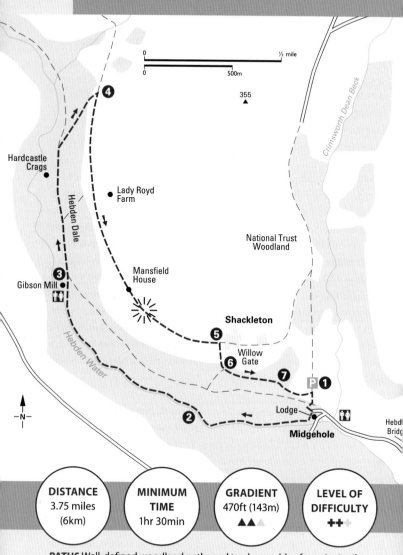

0 ½ mile

0 500m

355 ▲

4

Hardcastle Crags

Hebden Dale

● Lady Royd Farm

National Trust Woodland

Crimsworth Dean Beck

3
Gibson Mill ●

● Mansfield House

Hebden Water

Shackleton

5

6 Willow Gate

7

P **1**

Lodge

2

—N—

Midgehole

Hebden Bridge

DISTANCE	MINIMUM TIME	GRADIENT	LEVEL OF DIFFICULTY
3.75 miles (6km)	1hr 30min	470ft (143m) ▲▲▲	✚✚✚

PATHS Well-defined woodland paths and tracks, muddy after rain; 1 stile
LANDSCAPE Wooded gritstone valley floor and farm tracks
SUGGESTED MAP OS Explorer OL21 South Pennines **START/FINISH** Grid reference: SD 988291 **DOG FRIENDLINESS** Dogs should be under control at all times and on lead outside the woodland **PARKING** Pay-and-display at New Bridge car park (free for National Trust members), Midgehole, accessible off A6033, Keighley Road, Hebden Bridge **PUBLIC TOILETS** In Midgehole Road, near the start, and at Gibson Mill on route **NOTE** Modest admission fee to Gibson Mill

WALK 39 DIRECTIONS

❶ From the non-member pay-and-display car park at Midgehole, walk back to the main drive. Turn left towards the lodge but, at a finger post indicating the Mill Walk and the Picnic Area, turn right to the riverside path. Head right, upstream, following coloured waymark flashes painted on the trees. The path follows the riverside, occasionally rising above it. At a fork reached after 0.25 miles (400m) head left down stone steps to a level area of semi-mature Scots pine.

❷ The path continues in similar fashion, staying on the same river bank, ignoring any opportunities to cross on stepping stones and staying left where other paths are encountered. A mile (1.6km) beyond the car park, you reach Gibson Mill, where there are eco-friendly toilets, a friendly café and an excellent visitor centre.

❸ Continue up the valley, away from the stream's edge now, on the roughly surfaced vehicle track to the right of the mill, passing the disabled car park and wood store. The gritstone outcrops after which the property is named are passed on the left. Ignore the fork left 650yds (594m) beyond the mill and continue uphill for a further 0.25 miles (400m) to emerge from the woodland at a junction.

❹ Turn sharp right here on a roughly surfaced track signed 'Hardcastle Crags Via Shackleton'. Follow the level track for 1.25 miles (2km) past four farms, including Lady Royd Farm, the first building passed on your left.

❺ Just before entering Shackleton, pass through a metal field gate on your right, by a Public Footpath sign, into a field. Follow the wall on your left for 20yds (18m), then turn left down a short, boulder-choked walled lane to a rotting stile. Over the stile, turn left along the edge of the woodland.

❻ An old flagged causey path, buried in places beneath centuries of leaf mould, leads you back into the woodland. Immediately ignoring a trail to the right, just beyond is a boulder known as Slurring Rock.

❼ The descending path carries you past the barely noticeable ruins of Winter Well and delivers you back into the car park.

🍴 EATING AND DRINKING

The family-friendly Muddy Boots Café at Gibson Mill offers simple fare such as soup, sandwiches and cake. Although dogs aren't allowed inside, there's an area for them outside – they even get a welcoming dog biscuit! The café is open daily between March and October, except for Mondays and Fridays, and weekends from November to the end of February.

STOODLEY PIKE

A monument to peace surrounded
by the largest sponge imaginable.

It might not look like your typical agricultural landscape, but without the bounties harvested from the peaty uplands of West Yorkshire, and elsewhere, life would be very difficult indeed.

The moorland peat acts as a gigantic reservoir, absorbing and retaining millions of gallons of water like a giant sponge. The reservoirs that mankind has built on those uplands really serve as combine harvesters, collecting water as it slowly drains from the peat and siphoning it off into a system of pipes and treatment works for drinking, washing and for industry.

Peat – A Miracle Substance.

Without peat, the rain would simply run off the moors, lost to the water companies and causing regular, severe flooding in the process. It is formed by partially decayed moorland vegetation, principally sphagnum moss; the wetter the moor, the faster the peat forms, though it is a slow process.

Britain's peaty uplands, especially the Pennines, are also the equivalent of our own rain forest, as peat is a natural carbon sink, trapping up to 5,000 tonnes of carbon in every 2.5 acres (1ha). Take away the peat, and there are even fewer checks on global warming.

In the past peat moorlands have traditionally been 'gripped' – drained by ditches – to improve habitat for game birds or to allow forestry planting. The more recent realisation that this was causing flooding downstream of the sites due to faster water run-off, as well as degradation of habitat for wild ground nesting birds, has seen a widespread reversal of the practice and the old grips are being blocked up in many areas. So important are the moors of West Yorkshire for birdlife that many have been given European protection as part of the South Pennines Special Protection Area.

That's all hard to appreciate when you're crossing a sodden moor and you suddenly slip knee-deep into a bog. But it alls serves as warning for this, possibly the muddiest walk in the book. If you do find your boots filling up with a foul-smelling, ruddy ooze, just contemplate its importance and take solace in the anticipation of a luxurious bath when you get home.

Opposite: A traditional causey path near Stoodley Pike

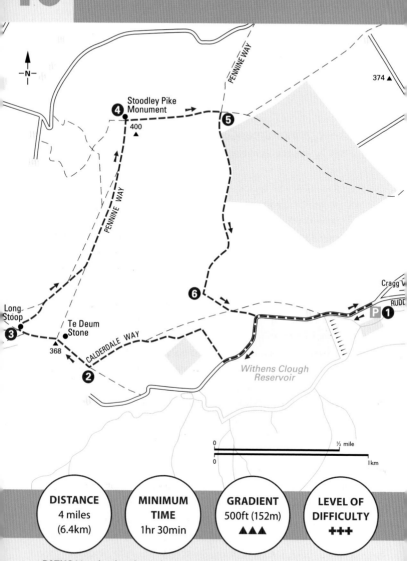

4 miles
(6.4km)

MINIMUM TIME
1hr 30min

GRADIENT
500ft (152m)
▲▲▲

LEVEL OF DIFFICULTY
+++

PATHS Moorland paths and rough pastures – plenty of opportunity for mud; 2 stiles **LANDSCAPE** Exposed peaty moorland, often wet **SUGGESTED MAP** OS Explorer OL21 South Pennines **START/FINISH** Grid reference: SD 986232 **DOG FRIENDLINESS** Under close control near livestock **PARKING** Withens Clough car park, Rudd Lane, Cragg Vale **PUBLIC TOILETS** None on route **NOTE** If the car park is closed for reservoir maintenance, park near St John's in the Wilderness Church in Cragg Vale and walk up Rudd Lane. A well-signed diversion should cover the first 220yds (201m) of the route. This adds 1.6 miles (2.7km) to the walk

WALK 40 DIRECTIONS

1 Turn left out of the car park, through a gate and along the track beyond, past the embankment of Withens Clough Reservoir and a farmhouse. Ignore the first path to the right and take the track 600yds (549m) beyond the farmhouse, signed 'Calderdale Way'. Leave this track and the Way after just 240yds (219m), bearing left to pass through a gate, winding along the top side of a small plantation. The Calderdale Way soon rejoins from the right and the track continues a further 340yds (310m) to a crossroads.

2 Bear right here, spurning a walled lane ahead to stay with the Calderdale Way to a gate by the inscribed Te Deum Stone. The track continues across open country beyond the gate; keep right when it forks, to follow causey stones, to a crossroads of paths by a 7ft (2.1m) tall obelisk known as Long Stoop.

3 The stoop marks the point at which you turn right on the Pennine Way along the edge of Langfield Common, which brings you to Stoodley Pike.

4 The Pennine Way bears right here. Stay with it for a further 550yds (503m), past a spring, the Slake Trough, to pass through a stone gap stile. Just beyond, the Pennine Way bears left over a wall, bound, ultimately, for Scotland. You, however, turn right, across the field, and pass through a stone stile in the wall opposite.

5 Follow the wall on your left. The path briefly becomes a narrowing walled track before crossing open country towards Withens Clough Reservoir. Yellow-topped poles guide you through a wet, reedy area and over a tiny wooden footbridge. You should then bear immediately right, over to a pair of stone gate posts and into a walled lane. This is sometimes so wet as to be impassable. Instead, parallel it in the pasture to its right, where another small footbridge eases passage across the boggiest bit. Enter the lane at a point at which it looks acceptably dry (accept, though, that your boots will get wet!). When the walls fade away, more yellow topped markers guide you over a third small footbridge to a walled enclosure, from which several paths depart.

6 Take the lowest path, signed 'To Withens Clough', cutting a diagonal line across pasture toward another fingerpost by the wall below. Go through the wall and turn left along your outward track to the car park.

Walking in Safety

All these walks are suitable for any reasonably fit person, but less experienced walkers should try the easier walks first. Route finding is usually straightforward, but you will find that an Ordnance Survey map is a useful addition to the route maps and descriptions.

RISKS

Although each walk here has been researched with a view to minimising the risks to the walkers who follow its route, no walk in the countryside can be considered to be completely free from risk. Walking in the outdoors will always require a degree of common sense and judgement to ensure that it is as safe as possible.

- Be particularly careful on cliff paths and in upland terrain, where the consequences of a slip can be very serious.
- Remember to check tidal conditions before walking on the seashore.
- Some sections of route are by, or cross, busy roads. Take care and remember traffic is a danger even on minor country lanes.
- Be careful around farmyard machinery and livestock, especially if you have children with you.
- Be aware of the consequences of changes in the weather and check the forecast before you set out. Carry spare clothing and a torch if you

are walking in the winter months. Remember the weather can change very quickly at any time of the year, and in moorland and heathland areas, mist and fog can make route finding much harder. Don't set out in these conditions unless you are confident of your navigation skills in poor visibility. In summer remember to take account of the heat and sun; wear a hat and carry spare water.

On walks away from centres of population you should carry a whistle and survival bag. If you do have an accident requiring the emergency services, make a note of your position as accurately as possible and dial 999.

COUNTRYSIDE CODE

- Be safe, plan ahead and follow any signs.
- Leave gates and property as you find them.
- Protect plants and animals and take your litter home.
- Keep dogs under close control.
- Consider other people.

For more information on the Countryside Code visit:
www.naturalengland.org.uk/ourwork/enjoying/countrysidecode